Becoming a Higher Level Teaching Assistant: Primary Mathematics

The Professional Teaching Assistant

Becoming a Higher Level Teaching Assistant: Primary Mathematics

● **Debbie Morgan**

Learning Matters

Every effort has been made to trace copyright holders and to obtain their permission for the use of copyright material. The author and publisher will gladly receive any information enabling them to rectify any error or omission in subsequent editions.

First published in 2006 by Learning Matters Ltd.

British Library Cataloguing in Publication Data
A CIP record for this book is available from the British Library.

ISBN 10: 1 84445 043 0
ISBN 13: 978 1 84445 043 5

Project Management by Deer Park Productions
Cover design by Code 5 Design Associates Ltd
Typeset by Pantek Arts Ltd, Maidstone, Kent
Printed and bound in Great Britain by Bell & Bain Ltd, Glasgow

Learning Matters Ltd
33 Southernhay East
EXETER EX1 1NX
Tel: 01392 215560
info@learningmatters.co.uk
www.learningmatters.co.uk

Contents

Introduction

HOW TO USE THIS BOOK

The focus of this book is mathematics. Together with the others in the *Becoming a Higher Level Teaching Assistant* series it has been designed not only to assist you in achieving Higher Level Teaching Assistant (HLTA) status, but also to encourage you to reflect upon and learn about the requirements of working in today's classrooms. Working in schools is a rewarding, though often challenging experience. The provision of high-quality learning experiences to all pupils in a class makes demands upon teachers and teaching assistants with regards to assessment, planning, classroom management and the development of teamwork. The role of the professional teaching assistant (TA) has gradually emerged over the past 30 years as a critical one in providing essential support to teachers and enabling all pupils to gain from a positive learning experience. Thomas, writing in 1992, suggests that over a ten-year period (1980–1990) many adults appeared in classrooms to work alongside teachers as a result of changes in schools which included a recognition of the need to address a wider range of special educational needs in classrooms, and an acknowledgement of the critical role which parents and other adults could play in supporting children's learning. Thomas further suggests that the arrival of more adults in the classroom has required that we reconsider the roles played by teachers and others, including TAs, and develop more effective ways of developing classroom teams. The recognition of the role of HLTAs may be interpreted as one important step in ensuring that we develop classroom teams in a way which is conducive to the effective learning of all pupils.

Many adults lack confidence in their understanding of mathematics. If you are one of those people you are not alone. The aim of this book is to support you as a TA to develop your confidence and expertise in the subject and enable you to support pupils more effectively in their mathematics learning. For this purpose some chapters have a specific mathematics focus with the aim of developing your own subject knowledge and confidence. These chapters are relevant for those supporting mathematics within all key stages in the primary school. It is a misconception to believe that good subject knowledge is only required by those working with older pupils. Effective supporters of learning will have secure subject knowledge of the mathematics that comes before and after the key stage in which they are working. Every broad area of mathematics is given some coverage, including number; shape, space and measures; data handling; and using and applying mathematics. Greater depth is included in some areas, either because they are considered difficult or to have greater importance. Using and applying mathematics has a central emphasis within Chapter 2 and is referenced throughout the book. A whole chapter is devoted to fractions, decimals, percentages, ratio and proportion as this is an area which many children and adults struggle with. The topic of data handling is included in the chapter on ICT as there are specific issues which relate to its use and the application of ICT. The chapter on shape, space and measures includes support for your knowledge of the properties of shape, progression in shape and the connections between number and measures. These are key and important aspects, which can sometimes be overlooked. Chapter 1 does not have a specific mathematics focus but provides an introduction to all of the HLTA standards. Practical strategies to support the teaching and learning of mathematics are explored throughout the book. Reference is made to your working relationship with teacher(s) and how this can be mutually supportive for developing pupils' learning. This book takes the view that effective mathematics learning enables pupils to understand mathematics in the sense of not just knowing what to do, but knowing why it works. A real understanding of mathematics provides opportunities for pupils to build on success and make connections within and across areas of mathematics, while developing confidence and enjoyment of the subject. You may not have had this experience in your own learning of mathematics, but I am sure you wish to provide a positive experience for the pupils you support. The aim of this book is to support you in achieving this goal.

This book is written in recognition of the fact that the important role played by TAs in our schools and colleges is finally being acknowledged, and that increasing numbers of TAs are seeking further training, qualifications and status within their schools. Some of the TAs who progress to HLTA status will go on to train as teachers through one of the many routes now available to them. Others will be satisfied to have had their professionalism recognised through the assessment process. Within this book I have endeavoured to recognise the major professional contribution which TAs make to schools and to provide a text which I hope will be of value to professional colleagues whichever route they choose to pursue.

This book uses a series of practical tasks and case studies to assist the reader in developing their own understanding of mathematics and analysing those factors which may influence the success or failure of learners in a typical classroom. Each chapter has a brief introduction, which is followed by an outline of the HLTA standards to be considered within the chapter. Inevitably, some of the standards will be addressed in more than one chapter, while others are very focused and may only be considered at a specific point in the book. Not every standard will be addressed, only those which relate to learning within mathematics. Early in each chapter you will find a box which outlines what you should have learned once you have read the chapter and completed the tasks within it.

The case studies have all been drawn from my own experience and those of colleagues and students with whom I have worked, although names and some details have been changed to preserve anonymity. These case studies are presented as a means of illustrating principles discussed in the chapter. You may consider these in respect of your own experiences and should always try to reflect upon them in a way that enables you to think about how you would deal with situations in your own school.

The practical tasks provided are designed to encourage you to reflect on your own practice, understanding of mathematics and the learning process. They have all been tried and tested by TAs enrolled on the Foundation Degree in teaching and learning at the University of Northampton.

At the end of each chapter you will find a summary of key points which indicates some of the most important principles discussed and which you may wish to consider in respect of your own practice and that of others within your school. A list of references and resources is also provided to support you in any aspects you may wish to peruse in greater detail to support your work in school and prepare you for HLTA status.

References

Thomas, G. (1992) *Effective Classroom Teamwork: Support or Intrusion?* London: Routledge

1. Meeting the Standards for the Higher Level Teaching Assistant

This book has been written with the aim of helping you to prepare for the new status of the Higher Level Teaching Assistant (HLTA) and focuses on the curriculum area of mathematics. It may be that you wish to cite mathematics or numeracy as a specialist area in your HLTA assessment or you just want to improve your competence and confidence in this area of the curriculum. It will also be valuable to those who simply want to improve their practice in supporting mathematics or who are enrolled on foundation degrees.

In the publication *Time for Standards* (DfES 2002), the government set out its plans for the reform of the school workforce. This reform recognised that support staff can, and do, make an increasingly critical contribution to all aspects of the successful operation of schools. At the same time there was an important acknowledgement that with training and support many teaching assistants (TAs) can operate at a higher level than may have been recognised in the past.

The HLTA Standards were published in September 2003 (TTA 2004) and identified those skills, and the understanding you will need to demonstrate in order to be awarded the status of HLTA. Many TAs when they first look at these Standards suggest that they already meet many, if not all, of them. You will find when we look at the Standards in detail that this is often the case but some standards may be more problematic to demonstrate than others. This may be because of the specific situation in which you have been working, or related to a lack of training in respect of certain elements of the standards. However, the key point to understand is the status of HLTA is awarded by the Training and Development Agency for Schools (the TDA, formerly the Teacher Training Agency (TTA)) via a number of Approved Training Providers and you will need to provide evidence to them that you can meet all of the standards as detailed. The main focus of this chapter is to help you to become familiar with the standards and to help you prepare for this assessment. Not every Standard is applicable to the curriculum area of mathematics but many are and reference is made to these throughout the book.

Assessment of HLTA status

There are a number of underlying principles which inform the assessment of HLTA, and these can be identified under the following headings.

- School support for the candidate
- Proficiency in literacy and numeracy (see Standard 2.6)
- Assessment must be manageable, rigorous and fit for purpose
- Assessment must take no more time than is necessary to demonstrate competence
- Assessment should be based on work that occurs during the normal course of duties
- It is the responsibility of the candidate to record evidence in support of the assessment.

The first of these principles is important for anyone contemplating going forward for assessment. The support of the school is essential if you are to be able to gather all of the evidence which you require in order to demonstrate that you meet the required Standards. Your head teacher will have to agree to your application to go on the HLTA route. It is also helpful to discuss this procedure with your immediate work colleagues who you will be asking to support you at various stages of the process. It is equally essential that at this stage you have a literacy or numeracy qualification at NVQ level 2 or its equivalent, as you will not be able to proceed successfully without this crucial evidence. Details of what constitutes these levels are available from the TDA website **www.tda.gov.uk**. The aim of the HLTA programme is that the assessment process should be linked to your normal workload; in other words, you should be in a position to use evidence from your daily working practice in order to support the assessment process. This aim, while laudable, has not in most cases, been realised and the majority of candidates have undertaken a large amount of additional work to ensure that they gain sufficient evidence to satisfy the assessors.

There are three routes to achieving HLTA status:

1. Assessment-only route: this is a three-day route spread over a term and is for more experienced TAs who feel that they already meet the Standards.
2. Training route: this provides face-to-face training. The length and nature of training are based upon a needs analysis. Candidates will opt into the training sessions they require. This route is for TAs who need training in certain Standards before they apply for HLTA status.
3. Specialist HLTA routes for candidates working within just one curriculum area within a secondary school.

An early priority must be to decide which is the best route for you. This depends on your current level of expertise and training and your personal confidence in relation to the HLTA Standards. This is where having the support of colleagues in school may be particularly helpful in providing you with an opportunity to discuss how both you and they feel about your current experience and expertise. If you have limited experience of working in schools as a TA and have undertaken very limited training, you need to explore how you can extend your knowledge and experience and then apply to go on the HLTA route in the future. If you feel that you need further training in order to meet the Standards, for example in the areas of SEN (special educational needs) or ICT (information and communications technology), then a training route is likely to be the most appropriate for you. As mentioned above, this is based on a needs analysis and you will select the relevant training sessions. This will be provided through face-to-face training and e-learning, using a computer.

If you feel that you have considerable knowledge, experience and skills related to the HLTA Standards you should apply to go on the assessment-only route. However, it would be advisable that before making this decision, you examine the HLTA Standards carefully to ensure that you are familiar with these, and will be able to provide clear evidence of your ability to meet them in assessment. The task at the end of this chapter is designed to enable you to do this.

The specialist HLTA route is aimed at TAs working in secondary schools, particularly where they are only supporting within a single curriculum area. At the time of writing, this route is in the early stages of development. Another possible route to HLTA is for those students who are taking a foundation degree or similar degree course. The increase in opportunities to undertake foundation degrees has, in many instances, been welcomed by TAs as enabling them to further their own professional knowledge and skills. You will still need to apply for a place on the HLTA via your local LEA and undertake the assessment-only route.

There are a number of stages for you to go through and some TAs reading this book will already be on an HLTA programme, while others are considering applying .The six stages for the three-day assessment route can be seen below.

- Candidate information

- Two-day briefing

- Assessment tasks

- One-day briefing and review

- School visit

- Decision communicated

It is possible to suggest that in the examples provided, John should take a training route, Angela an assessment course and Susan needs to opt for the assessment-only route as she is undertaking a foundation degree. However, much

PRACTICAL TASK

Consider the position of the following teaching assistants who are considering being assessed for the HLTA. Which of the three assessment routes would you recommend to them and why?

Susan is a TA currently working within the Foundation Stage. She is currently working towards a Foundation Degree for Teaching Assistants and hopes to achieve Qualified Teacher Status after she is awarded an honours degree. There are two Reception classes in the Foundation Stage in her school and Susan plans and delivers sessions on numeracy and creative developments. Susan works closely with the reception teacher. Susan wants to achieve HLTA status as a way of getting onto an employment-based route into teaching.

John is a TA who has worked in the school for one year and has an excellent awareness of autism spectrum disorders. He works with a Year 5 child who has a diagnosis of autistic spectrum disorder and now would like to expand his opportunities to work across the school with other groups of children.

Angela has undertaken a number of courses for TAs at her local university and worked as a Specialist Teaching Assistant for six years. She works with individual pupils, groups and a whole class for dance. She has experience of teaching dance to children and adults at her local community centre.

will depend upon the individual circumstances of the interested TAs as well as factors such as the support of the school in providing opportunities for gaining experience and the confidence with which they each approach the task. These are important factors which you need to consider in committing yourself to this process. Whichever route is most relevant to you, you will have to undertake the same assessment procedures as all the candidates on the other routes.

Motivation

It is essential that all TAs who approach the route towards gaining HLTA status consider those factors which motivate them to want to proceed. There are many reasons why you may wish to undertake this pathway.

Most experienced TAs like Susan and Angela would identify that their jobs have changed since they started. Susan is completing a Foundation Degree in Teaching and Learning and is using the HLTA status as a stepping stone to her ultimate professional goal of becoming a teacher. She has already identified an ambitious pathway which will ultimately lead her to further qualifications in order to join the teaching profession. Angela and John have not at present identified the HLTA as leading to a career move. Indeed, they both see the enhanced status of HLTA as their ultimate work-related goal. This, for many professional colleagues, will be sufficient in itself as a motivating factor in undertaking the HLTA pathway. The HLTA is not intended as a stepping stone towards gaining a teaching qualification, though some colleagues may find that it is a useful starting point for attaining a place on further training courses which may lead to this goal. Whatever your motivation for embarking on the HLTA, you are beginning a process which will lead to a recognition of your professionalism and will be recognised across educational institutions as an acknowledgement of your skills, knowledge and understanding.

Understanding the HLTA Standards

The HLTA Standards have been designed as a means of assessing your skills, knowledge and understanding as a professional and are divided into three sections:

1. Professional values and practice: 1.1–1.6
2. Knowledge and understanding: 2.1–2.9
3. Teaching and learning activities; these are further subdivided into:
   a) Planning and expectations: 3.1.1–3.1.4
   b) Monitoring and assessment: 3.2.1–3.2.4
   c) Teaching and learning activities: 3.3.1–3.3.8

You will be aware of these Standards if you have begun the application process. It is likely that on viewing these you may feel that some are fairly straightforward while others are more complex. It is probable that some standards will require some clarification. For example, standard 2.7 is *They are aware of the statutory frameworks relevant to their role.* With this Standard there is a need to specify the extent of the knowledge and understanding expected of TAs working at HLTA level. It is important to specify what is expected of their role and how this expectation will change from, for example, a TA working in a Year 6 class to one working in a nursery school. It is quite probable that you may be more familiar with some of the statutory requirements which relate directly to your current role. For example, if you are working as a TA supporting pupils with special educational needs, you may well feel quite conversant with the Special Educational Needs Code of Practice (DfES 2002). However, you may be less familiar with other statutory requirements. The important expression in standard 2.1 relates to *'frameworks relevant to their role'*. There will not be an expectation that you know every piece of educational legislation, but assessors will expect that you can demonstrate an understanding of those which have a direct bearing upon your professional performance.

In the publication *Guidance to the Standards* (TTA 2004) it was noted that

> *Support staff meeting this standard will be able to demonstrate they are aware of the legal framework that underpins teaching and learning, and broader support and protection for both pupils and adults. Whilst it is not necessary to for them to have a detailed knowledge of the whole legal framework they will be aware of their statutory responsibilities and where to gain information, support and assistance when they need it.*

(p 17)

There are, of course, policies and statutes which relate to critical elements such as child protection, of which all professionals working in schools need to have a good working knowledge.

Some standards contain a number of composite statements, for example standard 1.1:

> *They have high expectations of all pupils; respect their social, cultural, linguistic, religious and ethnic backgrounds; and are committed to raising their educational achievement.*

It may be that you work in a situation where there are few, or indeed no children for whom English is an additional language, and that there is little cultural diversity within your school. This cannot to be taken as a reason for not being aware of your responsibilities or for demonstrating your ability to meet this particular standard. It is quite possible that in the future the nature of your school population may change, or having gained your HLTA status you move to a different school with a more diverse population. It is therefore important you demonstrate that you can meet this standard in full.

Other standards may be specific to your working situation in other ways. For example, standard 2.2 states that:

> *They are familiar with the school curriculum, the age-related expectations of pupils, the main teaching methods and the testing/examination frameworks in the subjects and age ranges in which they are involved.*

If you are working in a junior school it is to be expected that you are familiar with the requirements of the National Curriculum for pupils working in Key

Stage 2. However, it would be reasonable to expect you to have some understanding of the requirements and content from the National Curriculum at both Key Stages 1 and 3, as there may be pupils in your school who as a result of special educational needs or being gifted or talented may be working outside of the programmes of study for their chronological age. In some instances, in your role as a TA you may be supporting pupils in a specific area of the curriculum such as literacy or numeracy and have little input into other subject-based lessons. You will, however, be expected to demonstrate an understanding of broader curriculum requirements for the age range with which you are working.

Familiarity with the standards is essential if you are to succeed in providing sufficient evidence to go through the assessment process. You should make full use of the *Guidance to the Standards* document, which will clarify interpretation of these and provides some useful exemplars. It is equally important that you seek the advice of experienced colleagues in your school who may be able to provide clarification with regards to school policies and point you in the direction of useful information.

The HLTA standards are demanding and it would therefore be surprising if you did not find that you needed to improve your work in relation to some of these. This book will not cover all of the standards but only those which impact on the mathematics curriculum and teaching and learning in a general sense. It will assist you in attaining the standards, but cannot act as a substitute for your own efforts in gaining information through your school and by engaging in professional discussion with your colleagues. Clearly, if you are undertaking training related to the HLTA you should receive guidance and support from your tutors. However, as stated in the assessment principles, it is anticipated that you will keep your own detailed records in support of the assessment process.

Summary

- There are three main routes into HLTA and you need to consider carefully which is more appropriate for you.
- The support of your school and colleagues is essential in enabling you to make a smooth progress through this process.
- In order to achieve HLTA status you will need to complete a series of assessments which indicate that you have achieved the standards.

References

Department for Education and Skills (2002) *Time for Standards*. London: DfES

Department for Education and Skills (2002) *Special Educational Needs Code of Practice*. London: DfES

Teacher Training Agency (2004) *Professional Standards for Higher Level Teaching Assistants*. London: TTA

Teacher Training Agency (2004) *Meeting the Professional Standards for the Award of the Higher Level Teaching Assistant Status: Guidance to the Standards*. London: TTA

2. Mathematics in the National Curriculum and the National Numeracy Strategy Framework

Introduction

The National Curriculum programmes of study for mathematics and the National Numeracy Strategy Framework for teaching mathematics from Reception to Year 6 (NNS Framework) are two key documents which you need to be familiar with as a TA, supporting learning in mathematics. This chapter will explore these two key documents along with some other DfES publications which are relevant to your role as a TA.

Schools must meet the requirements of the National Curriculum in their delivery of the curriculum. Schools are not required to use the NNS Framework but are strongly recommended to do so as it is recognised as representing good practice. Most practitioners find it a valuable tool in providing detail to supplement the requirements of the National Curriculum. These documents will support you in recognising age-related expectations. They will also enable you to monitor progression in learning and provide feedback to the teacher.

HLTA STANDARDS

2.2   They are familiar with the school curriculum, the age-related expectations of pupils, the main teaching methods and the testing/examination frameworks in the subjects and age ranges in which they are involved.

2.3   They understand the aims, content, teaching strategies and intended outcomes for the lessons in which they are involved, and understand the place of these in the related teaching programme.

2.7   They are aware of the statutory frameworks relevant to their role.

3.2.1 They are able to support teachers in evaluating pupils' progress through a range of assessment activities.

CHAPTER OBJECTIVES

By the end of this chapter you should:

- understand the nature of the National Curriculum for mathematics and the NNS Framework and the relationship between them
- understand the nature of the Curriculum Guidance for the Foundation Stage
- understand the importance of using and applying mathematics within the National Curriculum
- understand the purpose of intervention programmes for mathematics and the role of the TA in the delivery of these materials.

The National Curriculum

The National Curriculum for mathematics, as with all subjects, is broken down into two parts, programmes of study and attainment targets. The programmes of study outline what is to be taught for Key Stage 1 to Key Stage 4 and the attainment targets indicate the expected levels of attainment as pupils progress through each key stage.

It is important to note the numbering of the programmes of study for mathematics. Mathematics 2 (Ma2) is presented as the first programme, followed by Ma3 and then Ma4. There is no separate Ma1. The reason for this is that Ma1 used to be a separate strand before the National Curriculum was revised in 2000 and has been integrated into the other programmes. This element of mathematics is known as 'using and applying mathematics'. It is, however, assessed separately under Attainment Target 1 (AT1).

Ma2 and Ma3, with the addition of Ma4 for Key Stage 2, outline the knowledge, skills and understanding required to be taught:

> Ma2 Number
> Ma3 Shape, Space and Measures
> Ma4 Handling Data

Using and applying mathematics in the National Curriculum (AT1)

The opportunity to use and apply mathematics lies at the heart of successful learning in the subject. It is important that you are aware of the skills involved and allow them to impact on your everyday interactions with pupils. The National Curriculum outlines this area of mathematics under the headings of problem-solving, communicating and reasoning. As mentioned above, it is included within Ma2, Ma3 and Ma4. Its development does not have to be delegated to particular objectives, lessons or activities, but can and should be a part of any mathematics session. The skills for Key Stages 1 and 2 are summarised below with some suggestions on how you might include them in your daily support of pupils.

Problem-solving

- Make connections both within the mathematics curriculum and across other curriculum areas.
  You can prompt pupils to make connections with questions such as, 'do you remember that we did something similar last week when we were...?' or in a science lesson, 'do you remember when we drew a graph in the mathematics lesson?'
- Make decisions.
  You can involve pupils in decision-making through questioning, for example, 'can you think of another way of solving the problem or should we use a number line or a 100 square for these calculations?'

- Break down a more complex problem into simpler steps.
  Questions such as 'how shall we start?', or 'what shall we do first?' can prompt pupils to think about the problem and break it down into steps.

- Select and use appropriate mathematical equipment, including ICT.
  It may often seem easier for you to select and organise resources; however, pupils need opportunities to select their own resources. This could be from within a range that you have placed on the table.

- Approach a problem in different ways in order to overcome difficulties.
  Pupils need to understand that mathematics can be difficult sometimes and struggling to find a solution to a problem is part of a natural process. Support pupils through questioning, such as 'is there another way you could try?'

- Estimate and check results.
  You should regularly prompt pupils to estimate a result before calculating. Questions such as, 'what do you think the answer will be?'; 'will it be more than 100?'; 'how do you know it will be more than 100?' can be used to support pupils' thinking.

- Organise and work systematically.
  This is particularly relevant when working through an investigation such as 'how many different ways can you make ten?' Often pupils will work randomly at first; however, you can prompt them to organise their work through questions such as, 'how do you know you have found all the possibilities, could you sort them in order to check?'

Communicating

- Use the correct language associated with mathematics.
- Communicate in spoken, pictorial, symbolic and written form.
- Organise and refine ways of recording.
- Present and interpret solutions in the context of the problem.

The development of communication within mathematics is sometimes overlooked. As a TA working with individuals or small groups you can engage pupils in valuable discussions about their work; the strategies they have used, how they have presented it and how they might improve their recording. Also you have the opportunity to model and encourage pupils to develop correct mathematical vocabulary.

Reasoning

- Understand and investigate general statements.
  These might include such statements as 'the addition of two odd numbers is always even', or 'a multiple of ten always ends in zero'. These types of activities encourage pupils to look for connections within mathematics and give explanations for them. They may not be able to explain in precise mathematical language why, for example, the addition of two odd numbers results in an even number, but you can encourage them to reason and maybe demonstrate using resources. Connecting cubes, grouped in pairs,

can illustrate that the number five cannot be made without the addition of an 'odd' cube. This makes it an odd number. The combining of two groups of five, results in the 'odd' cubes joining to make a pair which demonstrates that the number is now even. Pupils can explore how this is true for any two odd numbers.

- Develop logical thinking and explain methods and reasoning.
  The opportunity to explain a piece of mathematics can encourage pupils to reason and think logically about their work. They should be encouraged to ask themselves the question 'does it make sense?'

- Recognise patterns and relationships and make predictions about them.
  Encourage pupils to look for pattern and recognise similarities and differences. Pattern occurs naturally in the environment, such as the pattern made by tiles on the floor or on the wheels of a car. Number patterns are also important, such as those created by counting in steps of five. This recognition of pattern will support pupils in making connections and developing understanding of the underlying structure of mathematics.

Pupils often need prompting to encourage them to reason and think about mathematics. Questioning is a key skill for you to develop in order to engage pupils in thinking and reasoning. It is a misconception to believe that lower-attaining pupils or those with special educational needs cannot develop reasoning skills. They may take longer, but it is worth persevering as without these skills their potential is limited.

The skills outlined above are process skills and as a TA you can have a significant influence on their development, in the type of support that you provide for pupils. It is very easy to support pupils to such an extent that you are almost doing the work for them. The suggestions made above should support you in developing learner independence and success in mathematics.

PRACTICAL TASK

- During the next week, use the table below to record the number of opportunities you use in your work with pupils to develop the skills for using and applying mathematics.

- You may not cover all of these skills in one week; at the end of the week consider whether there are any gaps that could have been addressed.

- Reflect on how much pupils are reliant on your support and how you could develop greater learner independence.

- This activity will help you to evaluate and improve your own practice. This is a requirement for your HLTA assessment.

	Using and applying mathematics	Make a note of the number of opportunities pupils have had to develop these skills
P R O B L E M S O L V I N G	Make connections both within the mathematics curriculum and across other curriculum areas	
	Make decisions	
	Break down a more complex problem into simpler steps	
	Select and use appropriate mathematical equipment, including ICT	
	Approach a problem in different ways in order to overcome difficulties	
	Estimate and check results	
	Organise and work systematically	
C O M M U N I C A T I N G	Use the correct language associated with mathematics	
	Communicate in spoken, pictorial, symbolic and written form	
	Organise and refine ways of recording	
	Present and interpret solutions in the context of the problem	
R E A S O N I N G	Understand and investigate general statements	
	Develop logical thinking and explain methods and reasoning	
	Recognise patterns and relationships and make predictions about them	

The NNS Framework

The National Numeracy Strategy (NNS) was introduced into schools in 1999. A key document accompanying the Strategy was the NNS Framework. It begins with an introduction which gives summary guidance on a range of issues, including the use of resources and supporting pupils with special educational needs and those with English as an additional language. Its main sections include *yearly teaching programmes* for each year group with lists of objectives to be addressed with exemplification of those objectives through *supplements of examples.*

Age-related expectations

The yearly teaching programmes in the NNS Framework act as age-related expectations for pupils. The attainment targets within the National Curriculum also provide expectations of what pupils should be able to do at the end of each key stage. The NNS Framework is probably an easier reference as it provides greater detail and does reflect expectations from the National Curriculum. Some pupils you work with, particularly those with special educational needs, will be working at below age-related expectations. It is important that you still have high expectations for their achievement. When working with them you should be aware of the age-related expectations and view the present objectives as a step towards them.

The supplements of examples provide greater clarity of expectations through specific examples of what pupils should be able to do. For those working below the expectations for Reception, a further document is available. *Towards the National Curriculum for Mathematics; examples of what pupils with special educational needs should be able to do at each P level* includes performance descriptions which illustrate progression. These are known as P levels and range from level 1 (P1) to level 8 (P8).

PRACTICAL TASK

- Select a learning objective from the NNS Framework that you have recently focused on in your work with pupils.

- Find the page that relates to this objective in the *supplements of examples* of the NNS Framework. Page numbers are given next to each objective in section three, 'the yearly teaching programme'.

- Track progression in this objective by looking at what is required for the area of mathematics in the year below and year above. This may be done by looking across the columns in the *supplements of examples*. If your pupils' age range spans Year 3 and Year 4 you will need to look at the relevant pages in both sections five and six of the Framework.

- This activity will allow you to reflect and gain an understanding of progression. You will need to demonstrate that you can evaluate progression as part of your HLTA assessment.

The NNS and the three-part lesson

The three-part lesson structure is a central theme of the NNS; it includes an oral and mental starter, the main part of the lesson and a plenary. The oral and mental starter, the introduction to the main part of the lesson and the plenary will normally be whole-class sessions. Your role during these sessions needs to be carefully considered and planned with the teacher. There are various roles that you can play to support the teacher in these whole-class sessions:

- Working alongside targeted pupils to keep them focused through repeating or rephrasing a question.
- Supporting pupils in calculation by encouraging the use of jottings or a resource such as a number line or a 100 square.
- Encouraging pupils to put their hand up to answer a teacher's question.
- Providing differentiation, maybe for higher attaining pupils; such as asking 'what is 5 multiplied by 60?' when the teacher has asked 'what is 5 multiplied by 6?'
- Carrying out assessments planned with the teacher through observation of pupils. The information observed can be recorded and fed back to the teacher.
- Scribing on the board or modelling a strategy using a resource, while the teacher gives an explanation.

The case study below illustrates how a TA supported pupils in the plenary part of the lesson.

Case study

Judy is a TA who regularly works with a small group of pupils in the daily mathematics lesson. These pupils are working at below age-related expectations and sometimes struggle to stay focused during the whole-class plenary. Judy prepares these pupils for the plenary by reminding them of what they have learnt. Once a month she helps them to prepare an activity to share with the rest of the class. On one occasion when the objective was to solve word problems, she supported the group in writing their own problems to challenge the rest of the class.

Reflection on the case study

These pupils were enabled to take part in the plenary session through Judy's prompting. The monthly activity developed their confidence and raised their self-esteem.

Curriculum guidance for the Foundation Stage

This document outlines an appropriate curriculum for children between the age of three and five. It is organised into six areas of learning, one of which is mathematical development. Age-related expectations are expressed in terms of 'early learning goals' and these are further broken down into 'stepping stones'. There is an overlap between the early learning goals and the objectives recorded for the Reception year in the NNS Framework. For those working in early years settings this is an excellent document and provides valuable guidance for the practitioner.

Other National Numeracy Strategy and DfES publications

There has been a wealth of publications offering guidance on a range of issues relating to the teaching and learning of mathematics. Some key documents related to the work of TAs are discussed below. Other materials are listed at the end of the chapter. The Primary Strategy website has a list of publications, most of which should be present in your school or can be ordered, usually free of charge.

Springboard Intervention Programmes

Springboard materials represent an intervention programme whose delivery is targeted at TAs who work with small groups of pupils outside of the daily mathematics lesson. The materials are aimed at pupils in Key Stage 2 working just below age-related expectations and their intention is to enable pupils to catch up and achieve level 4 by the end of Key Stage 2. Although detailed planning and resource materials are provided, it is important that you work with the teacher to ensure these meet the specific needs of the pupils who have been identified for this form of support.

Supporting children with gaps in their mathematical understanding: Wave Three mathematics

Wave Three materials are targeted at individual pupils who demonstrate fundamental errors and misconceptions in their mathematical understanding and are therefore not making sufficient progress in learning. The materials focus on common mathematical difficulties. It is likely that as with the Springboard materials they will be delivered by the TA. Unlike the Springboard materials, the intention is not to work systematically through them but to pick and choose according to the needs of individuals. In your everyday work with pupils be alert to their errors and possible misconceptions and provide feedback on these to the teacher. It may be that together you can identify materials from the Wave Three pack in order to address individual needs.

Case study

Cathy was responsible for delivering the Springboard 3 catch-up programme to a group of children in Year 3. They had reached unit 5, session 2. This required the children to count on in tens as an addition strategy. She knew from the previous lesson that children were still struggling with counting on in tens, so before the lesson she discussed this with the teacher, who suggested some practice and consolidation activities for the beginning of the lesson. Cathy used these and also adjusted the main part of the lesson to start with the addition of two multiples of ten, for example 40 + 30. This strategy was successful and she was then able to move on to working with pairs of numbers where one was not a multiple of ten, such as 43 + 30.

Reflection on the case study

This case study illustrates the need to adjust planning to meet the needs of pupils in order for progression in learning to take place.

Mathematical Vocabulary

It is useful for all TAs to have their own copy of this document. It provides a list of mathematical vocabulary for each year group, highlighting the introduction of new vocabulary as it appears. You need to be familiar with the expected vocabulary for the year groups in which you work and model its use for pupils. This is further discussed in Chapter 4. If you have difficulty obtaining a copy of this document, it is available to download from the Primary Strategy website, under 'publications'.

Special Educational Needs

Supporting pupils who may have difficulties accessing the mathematics curriculum because of special educational needs is given attention through a number of documents. These target specific needs such as autism, speech and language difficulties, hearing impairments, visual impairments, and those with dyslexia or dyscalculia. There is also guidance for pupils who have English as an additional language (EAL).

Summary

- Familiarity with the NNS Framework and its contents will provide you with a good overview of the curriculum in relation to mathematics and give you an understanding of age-related expectations. It will also support you in assessing pupil progress and providing feedback to the teacher.

- The importance of using and applying skills in mathematics cannot be underestimated. The support that you give to pupils can be invaluable in the development of these skills.
- It is useful to keep up to date with DfES publications. These can be accessed through your school or the Primary Strategy website.

References and resources

Curriculum Guidance for the Foundation Stage (May 2000), QCA Publications
www.qca.org.uk/223.html
Ref: QCA/00/587

Mathematical Challenges for Able Pupils in Key Stages 1 and 2 (June 2000)
Ref: DfEE 0083-2000

Mathematical Vocabulary (October 2000)
Ref: DfES 0313-2000

Towards the National Curriculum for Mathematics: Examples of what pupils with special educational needs should be able to do at each P level (September 2001)
Ref: DfES 0637-2001

Primary Education: Working with Teaching Assistants (February 2003)
Ref: DfES 0114-2003

Teaching Assistants File: Primary Schools (September 2003)
Ref: DfES 0586-2003

Mathematics Module: Induction Training for TAs in Primary Schools (August 2004)
Ref: DfES 0572-2004

Raising Standards in Mathematics: Achieving children's targets (December 2004)
Ref: DfES 1075-2004

National Numeracy Strategy: Supporting pupils with English as an additional language (March 2005)
Ref: DfES1438-2005WO

A Guide for Foundation Stage Practitioners (March 2005)
Ref: DfES1228-2005G

The Effective Management of Teaching Assistants to Improve Standards in Literacy and Mathematics (March 2005)
Ref: DfES 1228-2005G

Wave 3: Supporting pupils with gaps in their understanding (April 2005)
Ref: DfES 1168-2005G

3. The use of resources within the learning and teaching of mathematics

Introduction

Practical resources are routinely used to support the teaching and learning of mathematics. As a TA you will be involved in collaborating with the teacher to select and prepare resources to meet a variety of needs. It is important that you are aware of the resources that are available and how these can be used effectively to support learning.

> ### HLTA STANDARDS
>
> 3.1.3   They contribute effectively to the selection and preparation of teaching resources that meet the diversity of pupils' needs and interests.

> ### CHAPTER OBJECTIVES
>
> By the end of this chapter you should:
>
> - understand the purpose of resources to support pupils' learning in mathematics
> - know how to select and prepare resources to meet the needs of individual pupils
> - be able to use resources effectively to support learning
> - understand the mathematics behind some key structured resources.

Purpose of resources

The primary purpose of resources is to support and develop learning. In recent years the need to provide resources for kinaesthetic learners, who learn best through movement and manipulation, has received much attention. However, resources can be an asset to all pupils at different stages of learning. They can provide:

- **a visual image** which allows for the underlying structure of a mathematical concept to be seen with greater clarity; *for example, a 100 square enables the patterns within the place value system to be seen through its structure of rows and columns of ten. Multiples of ten appear in the same column, and the units digit in each column remains the same as the numbers increase by ten as you move down the columns.*
- **a support to calculation**: *for example, where a number line is used and the calculation broken down into manageable steps, and recorded as jumps*

along the line. *This supports the learner in keeping track of each stage in the calculation.*

- **a focus for discussion:** *for example, a picture or object providing a context for an area of mathematics.*

- **a tool for exploration and discovery:** *for example the use of construction materials to explore the properties of 3D shape.*

- **a stimulus to provide interest and interaction:** *for example, a class shop with money and priced items for purchase.*

Developing a positive attitude towards the use of resources

It is important that a positive attitude is developed towards the use of resources in classrooms and that all pupils appreciate and benefit from their use at certain times. They should not be viewed only as an aid for those who are experiencing difficulties in learning mathematics. When working with pupils of all abilities your use of resources can support the development of a positive attitude towards them. It is especially valuable for you to work alongside pupils in a role-play area or context, such as a shop. Here you can enrich the quality of the learning by modelling your own engagement with the mathematics involved, such as counting out your money to check if you have enough to buy an item, or by asking a pupil to check if you have given them the correct change.

Selection of resources

As a TA you may be asked by the teacher to select appropriate resources to support the learning of pupils with whom you are working. Alternatively you may realise that the resources you have been given to support a group of children are inadequate or inappropriate in relation to their specific needs. In discussion with the teacher you may suggest alternative resources. Key questions to consider when selecting a resource are:

- Does the resource support the learning objective?

- Is the resource age-appropriate? Expecting a Key Stage 2 child to count with teddies may be inappropriate.

- Is the resource selected the most appropriate for the mathematics involved? Counting on in ones or twos may be easier on a number line, whereas counting on in tens may be easier on a 100 square.

- Is the resource supporting learning and progression? The use of cubes may be encouraging counting in ones rather than developing mental strategies,

PRACTICAL TASK

- Select a game which you believe could be used to support learning in mathematics.

- Consider carefully which specific areas of mathematics it could address. Do not forget the skills and strategies involved in using and applying mathematics, discussed in the previous chapter.

- Could the game be adapted to provide differentiation and meet the individual needs of a group of pupils with whom you work?

- Play the game with a group of pupils and analyse whether it meets the objectives you identified and the extent to which it supports learning.

- This task will enable you to reflect on whether the resource is actually meeting the intended outcomes.

- As part of your HLTA assessment you will need to demonstrate that you are able to consider the learning needs and interests of the pupils with whom you work and select resources to meet those needs. Sometimes you may select a resource that you think will meet the needs of a pupil but after using it realise that it is not effective. This demonstrates your ability to reflect on your own practice and learn from experience.

Use of resources

The range and potential use of resources is vast. They can include the following:

- **Everyday objects**, such as buttons, shells, pasta for counting and sorting.
- **Mathematically structured resources**, such as number lines, and place value cards. These may be tailored to meet individual needs, such as limiting the numbers on the number line or removing the hundreds from the place value cards for a pupil who is in the early stages of exploring place value.
- **Games and puzzles** which practise and develop calculation and problem solving skills. The best games are often those made and designed by the TA who takes into consideration the interests and needs of the pupils.
- **ICT games and activities** which engage and motivate pupils in learning. There is a wealth of ICT software available, although careful selection is required to ensure learning takes place. Make sure you explore the software yourself first so that you are familiar with it and have thought about its potential as a learning tool.
- **Programmable toys** such as floor robots can be used to explore space, shape and distance and to develop logic and reasoning skills.
- **Construction materials** may be selected as a resource to explore 3D shape and its properties. A TA working alongside a group of children can support and develop the language of shape and space.

Seeking out new resources

Most primary classrooms have a variety of resources available for use; however, these may not be adequate to meet the diverse range of needs within any one class. Teachers will always be considering the potential of new resources. As a TA, working closely with some pupils, you may be able to contribute to these decisions through your own research. The internet is a potential source for research, providing information on a range of resources. A selected list of sites is provided at the end of this chapter. ICT itself is obviously a key resource and is discussed in detail in Chapter 9. Your school will have resource catalogues which you can browse through. Also talking to other teachers and TAs may generate ideas. This may be particularly valuable when considering a pupil with specific needs. Sometimes the resource may need to be created by you to meet those needs. The case study below illustrates this point.

> **Case study**
>
> *Tiro had just arrived in school. His family had just moved from Japan where he had lived all of his life. Karen, the TA, was delegated to support him in settling into the class and accessing the curriculum. He had very little English-language skills and Karen realised he had no number recognition, but she believed he could recognise numbers in Japanese. Karen used the internet to research images of Japanese numbers. She used these to design and make a number grid, matching Japanese to English numbers. Using this resource Tiro quickly learnt to recognise numbers and Karen discovered he was able to calculate with two digit numbers and was in fact a very able mathematician. He went on to teach the rest of the class how to count in Japanese.*
>
> Reflection on the case study
>
> *Karen not only enabled Tiro to access the mathematics curriculum but also enabled him to share his own expertise with the rest of the class. This helped him settle in and develop confidence in his new context.*

The potential of resources to support learning

Resources do not hold magical properties in the sense that a child given a resource to handle will immediately develop understanding. A resource is a tool to think with and the TA, working with an individual or small group of pupils, may be able to skilfully support that thinking through discussion and questioning in order to help pupils make sense of the mathematics involved. It is important to be aware that although the mathematics within a resource may be clear to you, this clarity may not be immediate to the pupil.

Using resources to enable pupils to take part in whole-class sessions

During whole-class elements of the daily mathematics lesson where the teacher is leading the session, you may use a resource to support an individual or group of pupils to take part. A pupil may be supported with a number line or a 100 square, to assist calculation during an oral and mental starter. A small whiteboard may also be useful to draw images to support pupils' thinking. You may also need to provide resources for pupils with special needs, for example, large digit cards for a pupil who has difficulty in seeing the board.

Resources to develop understanding of number and mental calculation

Some resources are mentioned specifically in the NNS Framework and are seen as key to developing pupils' understanding of number and success in mental calculation. These key resources are discussed in detail below. They require skilful handling if pupils are to receive maximum benefit from their use. It is important therefore that you understand their use, the mathematics they are intended to develop and any potential difficulties. This will enable you to be more effective as a TA in supporting learning.

Number lines

Number lines are a key mathematical resource for supporting calculation and developing an understanding of the underlying structure of the number system. They illustrate the ordinal nature of number and can be used as a powerful image to support calculation. Their use is discussed in detail in Chapter 5.

They come in a variety of shapes and forms, as listed below.

- Number tracks where the number occupies a space rather than a point on a line. These can be in the form of carpet tiles or a large number track on the floor. Pupils can then jump along the track counting as they progress. Electronic versions are also available which light up as pressure is applied.

1	2	3	4	5	6	7	8	9	10

- Number lines in their simplest form involving numbers 0 to 10 at regular intervals.
- Number lines which extend to larger numbers such as 0 to 100.
- Number lines including fractions and decimals.
- Number lines which extend to include negative numbers.
- Number lines which progress in steps, and only include multiples, for example

  0, 10, 20, 30, 40, 50

- Number lines showing intervals of time and other measures.
- Number lines which are blank and allow the child to scribe only the necessary numbers required for the calculation.
- Number lines sketched by pupils.
- Number lines which are presented in different orientations, such as vertical or are curved or even circular.
- Number lines which are imaginary. A useful activity is for you to step out an imaginary number line. Starting at zero, each step either represents one, or a multiple, and pupils are required to count your steps and identify the imaginary number you finish on. If you take five steps and you are counting in ones, the answer is five; if however you are counting in twos then the answer is 10. You need to make a clear to pupils the size of the step before you start.
- Number lines which are mental images.

If the pupils you are working with are not experiencing success in their use of number lines, it may be that they need a different form of number line or even a number track. This is a decision to make in discussion with the teacher. It may be that for a pupil with special needs, a larger number line is required where the numbers are not as close together. Where one is not available, you could make one, perhaps involving the pupil in its creation.

Number grids (100 square)

Number grids generally come in the form of squares with numbers that range from either 1 to 100 or 0 to 99. As a TA you will need to familiarise yourself with the square selected by the teacher. In the early stages it is preferable for pupils to be exposed to just one type. This may be different if you work with more than one class. It is therefore worth considering the distinctive features of both:

0 to 99 Grid	1 to 100 Grid
The multiples of 10 appear in the first column	The multiples of 10 appear in the last column
Zero is included, which provides opportunity for discussion of the concept	Zero is not included, which avoids a possible misconception, that zero has a tangible value as it occupies a square
	The square goes up to 100! This is motivational for many children

The opportunity may arise at a later stage to investigate other types of squares with pupils and make comparisons. For some pupils, perhaps those within the autistic spectrum, a square which starts with one in the bottom left-hand corner and moves up the grid with the larger numbers at the top, may be preferable. This decision needs to be made in discussion with the teacher.

Calculating using number squares

Number squares can provide support for calculation and the development of mental strategies. Ten or multiples of ten can be added or subtracted with relative ease by moving up and down the columns. This strategy can then be extended to the addition or subtraction of 9 and 11 by combining the up and down movement with a move to the right or left, so addition of 11 is one space down and then one space to the right. As discussed in Chapter 5, there is a danger that this can be just a procedural method, performed without understanding.

Working with 100 squares for calculation encourages pupils to reason the strategy for themselves, rather than simply following a sequence of instructions. This will help them to understand how the strategy works. It needs to be appreciated that there are ten numbers in each row and that by moving down one column a jump of ten has been achieved, even if this is from the middle of a row.

Should a number line or number square be used?

When working with pupils who need some support with calculation, you may need to make a decision whether a number line or number grid is preferable. Ideally and ultimately the pupils should make this decision for themselves. However you may prove to be a valuable support in helping in this decision-making process. For this purpose a comparison of both will be considered:

100 Square	Number Line
Easy to handle and position on the table	Can be long and unwieldy
Possible misconceptions in the language used. We talk about *moving down* one when adding ten. The word 'down' may be associated with numbers getting smaller, as in '*count down*'.	
Difficulties with movement, in reaching the end of a row and needing to move to the next subtraction	Movement is clear. Forward for addition, back for subtraction
Due to the positioning of the numbers, patterns in the structure of the number system are easier to identify	The linear nature of the number system is clear. Numbers continue one after the other and other numbers such as fractions and decimals can be placed in between. Also the number line can be extended in both directions to include negative numbers and numbers greater than 100
Addition of 10 is easy	Multiples of 10 may need to be highlighted to support calculation strategies

Both will prove valuable but at different times depending on the learning objective and the mathematics involved.

Place value grids

These align numbers to enable certain patterns in the number system to be exposed. They also provide opportunities for partitioning and combining the constituent parts of numbers. The position of the hundreds, tens and ones underneath each other (for example 6 is under 60, which is under 600) enables place value to be explored. The movement of the 6 to the left as the number increases by a factor of ten (60) and then by ten again (600) can also be highlighted and explored. Both class and individual charts can be used.

0	100	200	300	400	500	600	700	800	900
0	10	20	30	40	50	60	70	80	90
0	1	2	3	4	5	6	7	8	9

Place value is a key concept for success in mathematics. These grids may provide another resource for pupils with the potential for development of understanding. If they are not already used in your class, it may be worth considering their use in discussion with the teacher. You may suggest that you use them with a small group of pupils who require additional support in this area of mathematics. Activities are suggested below for their use.

Activities

Saying the number names: Point to one number from each row, starting at the top; pupils say the numbers in turn, for example 'four hundred' (as 400 is pointed to) and 'fifty' (50), 'four' (4). You need to highlight the insertion of '*and*' after the hundreds but not the ones.

Partitioning: Give a number in written form, for example 642; the pupils then have to place counters on 600, 40 and 2 and possibly record these numbers so that the number is viewed or written in its partitioned state.

Combining: Ask the pupils to place counters on numbers such as 200, 30 and 5. Ask pupils to then record what the number will look like in its combined state of 235.

Repetition of these activities should support the development of place value and provide opportunities for partitioning and combining numbers. This is a useful skill in mental calculation.

Place value cards

As with the above resource, these cards provide opportunities to partition and combine numbers and focus on place value. They allow for the physical manipulation of a number between its partitioned and combined state. In the illustration below 20 and 6 can be combined by placing one number on top of the other to form 26. In this state it can then be partitioned into its original state of 20 and 6.

Number cards

Number cards can be used as a resource in a number of different contexts. As discussed in Chapter 5, knowledge of number bonds is essential for success in calculation. Many of the lower-attaining pupils you work with may have a poor retention of number bonds. You can support individual pupils by making sets of number bond cards, starting with bonds to 10. Pairs of numbers totalling 10 are written on the cards, one number on each side, for example 4 and 6. Games can be played with the cards where a card is won if the paired number on the back is given correctly. Cards can be taken home for practice and more cards added as facts are learnt.

Arrays

Arrays are mentioned in Chapter 5 as a resource to support and develop understanding of the relationship between multiplication and division. They first appear in the NNS Framework in Year 2 as a resource to support understanding of the commutative property of multiplication: that 2×4, for example, produces the same result as 4×2. This mathematical idea could simply be presented to pupils as a fact to be remembered; however, it is of greater benefit if pupils understand why this works. This can be achieved through the visual form of an array. 2×4 is the same array as 4×2; both facts can be seen in the same array.

Here the groups of four are highlighted $2 \times 4 = 8$.

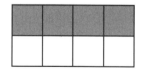

Here is the same array but with groups of two highlighted $4 \times 2 = 8$.

The array can also illustrate the related division facts of 8 divided into groups of 4, is equal to 2 ($8 \div 4 = 2$), and 8 divided into groups of 2 is equal to 4 ($8 \div 2 = 4$).

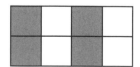

This resource provides a powerful image of some key mathematical ideas. However, these may not be grasped immediately by pupils. As you work alongside pupils, you should help to reinforce these ideas through questioning and discussion. Arrays can also be presented in a tactile form through the use of cubes, beads and partitioned trays.

Understanding of the mathematics involved in this simple visual image can support further development; particularly that of multiplication, as it leads into the use of the grid method which is illustrated in Chapter 5.

Withdrawal of resources

Although resources are a valuable learning aid, there is the danger that some pupils may become over-reliant on them. You can be involved in monitoring the use of resources by some pupils, and in discussion with the teacher make decisions relating to the withdrawal of a particular resource or the use of an alternative resource.

Case study

Bob, the TA, had been working with Paul, a Year 5 pupil, since the beginning of the academic year. Paul had learning difficulties and was working below age-related expectations at level 2A. Paul used a 0 to 100 write on/ wipe off number line for calculating. At the beginning of the year he was adding two-digit numbers by starting with the largest number and adding the smaller by counting along the number line in ones. He could now add by jumping along the number line in groups of ten and then ones. In order to develop further independence Bob suggested to the class teacher that he should attempt to remove the number line but replace it with a sketched number line to support calculation. At first Paul wanted to write down all the numbers on his sketched number line, which was laborious and time consuming, he also reverted to counting on in ones. But Bob persevered and persuaded Paul that he could still count in tens and need only write down these numbers in order to keep track of where he had got to in the calculation. The ones could then be counted on in his head and the final result recorded. Paul was soon able to calculate beyond 100 using this method.

Reflection on the case study
Withdrawal of the resource initially resulted in Paul's progress stagnating. In the longer term progress was made as Paul developed greater confidence in the use of the sketched number line. An additional benefit was that the resource was always available, even in a test situation.

Summary

- Resources can be valuable learning tools and may provide the means for a child to understand a concept or be involved in a lesson.

- Appropriate selection and preparation of resources, taking into account the needs of the learner and the mathematics involved, is crucial.
- Not all resources are valuable at all times; they require careful selection, taking the needs and development of learners into consideration.
- Decisions need to be made as to when a resource could be removed and maybe replaced with an alternative resource to ensure progression and the development of learner independence.
- It is useful for a TA to have their own bank of key resources on which they can draw to support learners who may be having difficulty at a particular point.

References and resources

These websites can be found by typing the title into a reliable search engine.

Mathsweb is Leicestershire's numeracy website and contains printable resources and ideas for their use.

Beam is an educational development organisation and publisher. They produce a variety of resources for purchase, including number lines, cards and games.

MathsNet is aimed at resources for Key Stage 2 and above. It provides a number of interactive games that can be played online.

NRICH is an online maths club for schools and provides mathematical challenges, games and puzzles.

Numeracy Software, provides a range of free downloadable software to support learning.

Count on provides a range of games puzzles and ideas for all ages.

Primary Maths Resources (games, activities and printable resources).

The Standards Site: Interactive Teaching Programs are useful ICT programs to explore and develop understanding of mathematics. They include a program that uses place value cards.

Association of Teachers of Mathematics provides a number of resources to purchase for all ages. These include a piece of software called 'Developing Number' which includes the use of place value cards.

Ambleweb is a website run by a primary school. It provides both printable and online interactive resources to support all subjects including mathematics. Some of the resources have been produced by pupils from the school.

Claire publications produces a variety of books and resources for purchase, including number lines and teddies.

Numeracy Resources CD Ansell, R. (2005)

This resource can be purchased from the following website: www.numeracycd.com It contains a large number of printable resources for Key Stages 1 and 2.

4. Inclusion and equality

Introduction

Every pupil has the right of access to the National Curriculum. TAs are often used as a means to ensure inclusion in the classroom through their targeted support of individuals or groups of pupils. In this chapter we shall consider potential barriers which may obstruct or deny full assess to the mathematics curriculum and how you, through your role as a TA, can make a contribution towards ensuring that appropriate opportunities are provided for pupils to progress and develop.

HLTA STANDARDS

1.1   They have high expectations of all pupils; respect their social, cultural, linguistic, religious and ethnic backgrounds; and are committed to raising their educational achievement.

1.2   They build and maintain successful relationships with pupils, treat them consistently, with respect and consideration, and are concerned for their development as learners.

1.3   They demonstrate and promote the positive values, attitudes and behaviour they expect from the pupils with whom they work.

3.3.1   They recognise and respond effectively to equal opportunities issues as they arise, including by challenging stereotyped views, and by challenging bullying or harassment, following relevant policies and procedures.

3.3.3   They promote and support the inclusion of all pupils in the learning activities in which they are involved.

CHAPTER OBJECTIVES

By the end of this chapter you should:

- recognise gender issues within mathematics
- understand the importance of language within mathematics, including provision of access for English as an additional language (EAL) pupils
- recognise some of the potential barriers to learning within mathematics
- appreciate the importance of high expectations and providing suitable support to enable inclusion and progression within mathematics
- recognise that mathematics is a universal language; however also appreciate that different cultures can bring individual aspects which enrich the curriculum.

Gender issues within mathematics

The view that *'boys are better at mathematics than girls'* is one that is still perpetrated in society. Unfortunately, this can become a self-fulfilling prophesy if those working and supporting in schools do not actively oppose this view and ensure they have equally high expectations of both genders. It is important that through your own attitude and behaviour towards both sexes you provide a positive role model. You need to challenge any stereotypical views that arise in your work with pupils and report these instances to the teacher. The case study below illustrates this point.

Case study

Lynda, a TA, was working with a small group of pupils in Year 4. They had been identified by the teacher as those who would benefit from the Springboard Year 4 intervention programme. There were five children in the group, four girls and one boy.

During the first session, most of the questions were answered by the boy in the group who was quick to arrive at solutions. One of the girls in the group noticed this and commented 'Sam answers all the questions, that's because boys are good at maths'. *Lynda responded to this by saying* 'girls are good at maths too'. *Lynda realised that she had overlooked the fact that Sam had answered most of the questions. She made a mental note to monitor and ensure that the girls in the group were actively encouraged and given time to answer questions in the next session. She also reported the comment to the teacher, who addressed the matter later in the week in a class assembly. The assembly focused on people who use mathematics in their jobs and gave examples of successful female mathematicians.*

Reflection on the case study

Lynda had overlooked the fact that she had allowed Sam to answer most of the questions. Once she had noticed, she addressed the issue. As a professional you are not going to perform perfectly all of the time. You will make mistakes; the important thing is that you learn from them. As part of your HLTA assessment you will need to demonstrate that you are able to improve your practice through self-evaluation.

Language in mathematics

Language is a key aspect within mathematics, which can have an impact on inclusion and success within the subject. The National Numeracy Strategy has placed a significant emphasis on its acquisition and development within curriculum. Key vocabulary is identified for each year group and published in a booklet and as a resource on flashcards. Teachers will identify key vocabulary for each lesson and topic and this may be displayed on the classroom wall. It is important that you know in advance the vocabulary for the lesson, so that you are able to successfully model its use when working with pupils. Research suggests that where language is modelled by TAs in the classroom this has a significant impact in its use by pupils. Not only are you supporting pupils in becoming familiar with the language but you are also developing their understanding of the language where you apply it to a relevant context.

Mathematics can be viewed as having a language of its own and requires precision in its use. There are some words which are almost exclusive to the subject, such as 'equation' and 'square root'. These need to be learnt and added to a pupils' vocabulary at the appropriate time. Others may be familiar words which are used in everyday language, but have a different meaning when applied to mathematics, such as 'table' and 'take away' (not the fish-and-chip variety!). It is important that you are aware of possible confusion and observe and question pupils to ensure that their understanding is secure. Most children enjoy learning new words and can master technical language; 'dodecahedron', for example is often a favourite word in Key Stage 2 classrooms.

Language is important in providing access to mathematics. It supports understanding of mathematical concepts and enables pupils to explain mathematical thinking. Children with whom you work may have poor language skills in general; however, this is not a reason for avoiding mathematical vocabulary. Explain vocabulary in everyday words and put it in context so that pupils develop understanding. Encourage pupils to verbalise and use mathematical language. Give praise where appropriate language is used and persevere where it is not. You can play a vital role in ensuring that language within mathematics is not a barrier to learning.

PRACTICAL TASK

The aim of this task is for you to explore mathematical vocabulary and consider some of the difficulties that may arise in the development of its use.

Using the DfES *Mathematical Vocabulary* booklet (see Chapter 2), identify the vocabulary for the year group(s) you work within.

- List those words which have a different meaning in mathematics than in everyday language.

- Research the meaning of any words you are unsure of.

- Identify the vocabulary for the next mathematical topic you will be supporting and be ready to use it.

- As part of your HLTA assessment you will need to demonstrate that you have high expectations of pupils; this includes their use of mathematical vocabulary.

Reflection on the task

You may have been surprised at the number of words you identified. These words are a potential source of confusion to pupils. You need to be aware of them in your work with pupils and ensure that they understand the vocabulary they are using.

You may find access to a good mathematical dictionary valuable (suggestions are included at the end of this chapter).

Accessing the mathematics curriculum where English is an additional language

Bilingualism is an asset and should be valued; however, it may cause a potential barrier to learning in the short term where English is being developed and needs to be considered. Often a TA may be asked to work closely with an EAL pupil with the aim of ensuring their access to the curriculum. Below is a list of guidelines to ensure effective support.

- Have high expectations of potential achievement. The English skills of a pupil may be weak at this point in time; but it does not necessarily follow that mathematics is also weak. Work in collaboration with the teacher to ensure appropriate mathematical challenge.

- Recognise that children have a propensity to acquire language skills much faster than adults. Encourage pupils' verbalisation of English and do not necessarily correct every mistake they make, as this may destroy their confidence.

- Some TAs are employed specifically because of their own bilingual language skills; if you do have language skills, make this known to pupils. For an EAL pupil, even if your language is not the same as theirs, knowing that others in the classroom speak other languages can be reassuring. Also it is important for all pupils in the class to be aware and respect other languages. Your own attitude towards these will impact on pupils and you can act as a positive role model.

- Ensure that pupils know that their language is valued by encouraging them to share elements with others in the class, maybe teaching a group to count to ten.

- Make use of visual elements such as number lines and 100 squares and use these to point out numbers the teacher is making reference to in the whole-class teaching elements of the lesson. Seeing where numbers fit in relation to each other can enable pupils to identify number patterns and develop their understanding of the number system.

- EAL pupils understand more than they can verbalise in English. Encourage them to communicate their understanding in other ways, maybe through drawings or the use of objects.

Supporting pupils with special educational needs

The aim of the National Numeracy Strategy is that all pupils should have access to the daily mathematics lesson. The guidance below is taken from *Guidance to support pupils with specific needs in the daily mathematics lesson* (DfES 2001). This document provides detailed and practical suggestions to enable pupils to access learning in mathematics. It is referenced at the end of this chapter and can be downloaded or ordered through the Primary Strategy website.

Visually impaired pupils require a far greater tactile experience of number, shape and measures to compensate for their limited visual experience.

Hearing-impaired pupils require greater exposure to the visual element of mathematics through the use of pictures, 100 squares, number lines, place value cards, digit cards, etc. Attention also needs to be given to the development of mathematical vocabulary to support understanding of concepts.

Pupils with speech and language difficulties need to experience the use of tactile apparatus as a thinking tool and to support their communication of ideas. Mathematical vocabulary needs to be introduced slowly and systematically.

Pupils with autistic spectrum disorders may find it difficult to join in with the whole-class and group elements of the daily mathematics lesson, such as counting. They should be allowed to be on the periphery of the group until they feel confident to take part. It should be remembered that lack of engagement does not indicate lack of knowledge or skills.

Dyslexia and dyscalculic learners may experience difficulty in counting, ordering and recognising pattern. Carefully structured activities which emphasise order and pattern will be supportive.

It is often tempting when working with pupils with special educational needs to lead them through a process, step by step, experiencing success at every juncture. All pupils need to be allowed to make mistakes. Pupils with special educational needs, like all pupils, should to be allowed to think for themselves and learn from their mistakes within a positive environment. As a TA you will get to know some pupils very well. You may recognise where pupils need additional support or resources to enable them to succeed. Working with the teacher you can make a valuable contribution to ensuring that individual needs are met and all pupils are given access to the mathematics curriculum and the opportunity to succeed.

High expectations and the mathematics curriculum

It is essential that all professionals working within a classroom have high expectations of all pupils. As a TA you are more likely to work with lower-attaining pupils. A high expectation of their potential achievement is important if they are to succeed. Too often children who are considered be lower attaining or have special educational needs are given repetitive or boring tasks in a mathematics lessons.

When working with individuals or small groups, monitor their engagement in tasks. Ask yourself: are pupils developing new understanding and making progress? This information can be fed back to the teacher and together you may be able to experiment and try alternative methods and activities to motivate pupils. Improved engagement may be the key to progression. The case study below illustrates this point:

Case study

The objective for the lesson was to know and use number bonds to 10 and 20. A small group of higher-attaining pupils were to work with bonds to 100 in the context of money, investigating totals that equalled £1:00 (100p). The middle group were to investigate pairs of numbers which totalled 10 and then 20. The challenge was to find as many ways as possible. The lower-attaining group with whom Lisa, the TA was working had a worksheet with a series of calculations to complete by filling in the empty box:

$$5 + 5 = \boxed{}$$
$$8 + 2 = \boxed{}$$

Cubes were provided to support the addition. Lisa made sure that each child got out the correct number of cubes for each calculation and counted them accurately. Having done the first couple, Tom guessed that they were all going to add up to ten. He got fed up counting his cubes and started flicking them across the table to Liam. Lisa recognised that the pupils were bored and so decided that she needed to do something to reengage and keep them on task. She took a pair of scissors from her bag and started to cut up Tom's worksheet. All the pupils in the group were so surprised that they stopped what they were doing and focused on Lisa. Lisa then placed all the cut number sentences on the table.

Lisa: I want to put these in a different order, to help us remember them, that's why I have cut them up.
Tom: Put 5 + 5 = 10 first.
Lisa: Why that one?
Tom: Because I know that one.
Lisa: Well why did you get out the bricks to work it out?
Tom: Because I thought we had to!
Lisa: Which shall we put next?
Annie: Put 6 + 4.
Lisa: Why?
Liam: Well, it's like when you're counting 6 comes after 5.
Lisa: Ok, using Annie's rule which one shall we put next?
Tom: 7 add 3.
This continued to 10 + 0 = 10.
Lisa: What comes next?
Liam: 11 add something.
Lisa: If you had 11 add something could the answer be 10?
Tom shrugged his shoulders.
Lisa: Let's get out 11 cubes.
But before 11 cubes had been selected . . .
Tom: No it won't work because we'll have too many.
Lisa: Where will 4 + 6 go?

Lisa expected pupils to say 'above 5 + 5'.
Liam: Next to 6 + 4.
Lisa: Why do you want to put it there?
Liam: Because it's the same.
Lisa then entered into a discussion with the group as to whether it was the same and agreed that it was a good idea to put it next to 6 + 4. Another useful discussion arose around the sentence 10 + 0.
Ashley: 10 + 0 is cheating.
Lisa: Why?
Ashley: Because you're not adding anything!
Lisa: You mean the number stays the same, so 10 add zero is 10.
Ashley: Yes, you're not adding anything!
Lisa: Can anyone give me any other examples of adding zero?
Carl: 8 + 0 is 8.
Mary: 100 + 0 is 100.
Liam: One hundred million million add zero is one hundred million million!
Number sentences were organised so that a pattern was evident:

$$5 + 5 = 10$$
$$6 + 4 = 10 \qquad 4 + 6 = 10$$
$$7 + 3 = 10 \qquad 3 + 7 = 10$$
$$8 + 2 = 10 \qquad 2 + 8 = 10$$
$$9 + 1 = 10 \qquad 1 + 9 = 10$$
$$10 + 0 = 10$$

After the lesson Lisa fed back to the teacher and together they built on Lisa's adjustment of the session to plan the next lesson.

Reflection on the case study

- *The organisation of the number bonds enabled pupils to begin to see patterns and connections between the number sentences. These patterns and connections support pupils in developing mental recall of number facts.*
- *Because of the arrangement of the bonds side by side the number of facts to be memorised was reduced by a half.*
- *Notice that Tom said he already knew that 5 + 5 = 10, but was still using cubes. Counting with cubes is laborious; there is the danger of lower-attaining pupils become dependent on their use.*
- *Lisa's adjustment of the session provided opportunities for the pupils to think, reason, discuss, make decisions and see connections. These are all important using and applying skills as discussed in Chapter 2 and are central to success in mathematics.*
- *Lisa provided appropriate challenge and the pupils responded to this. Imagine the feeling of satisfaction that Liam gained from knowing the answer to 100 million, million, add zero. Lisa mentioned this to the teacher and she gave Liam the opportunity to share this knowledge with the rest of the class during the plenary.*

Cultural diversity within mathematics

It is a misconception to believe that mathematics is the same all over the world. There are cultural differences in strategies for calculation and use of pattern, for example. Through your own knowledge and research you may be able to make some suggestions to the teacher for the inclusion of cultural diversity within mathematics. It is important to be aware, as pupils join the class from different countries, that they may use different methods and strategies. Value and encourage the sharing of these and support pupils in making links to the new strategies that they are being introduced to. The National Numeracy Strategy promotes the use of a range of strategies, particularly for mental calculation, and pupils' own strategies may be incorporated into these.

Summary

- Stereotyping of gender within mathematics may still be evident and this needs to be addressed by professionals working within education.
- Provision of a challenging and rich mathematics curriculum should be for all pupils. You can play your part in this by monitoring pupils' engagement and progression in tasks and providing feedback to the teacher. Working in collaboration you can support inclusion within the mathematics curriculum.
- Unfamiliarity with the language used within mathematics may deny pupils access to the curriculum. Your role within its development is important.

References and resources

Guidance to Support Pupils with Dyslexia and Dyscalculia (November 2001)
Ref: DfES 0512-2001

Guidance to Support Pupils with Visual Impairments (November 2001)
Ref: DfES 0510-2001

Guidance to Support Pupils with Hearing Impairments (November 2001)
Ref: DfES 0514-2001

Guidance to Support Pupils with Speech and Language Difficulties (November 2001)
Ref: DfES 0513-2001

Guidance to Support Pupils with Autistic Spectrum Disorder (November 2001)
Ref: DfES 0511-2001

Including all Children in the Literacy Hour and Daily Mathematics Lesson (November 2002)
Ref: DfES 0465-2002

Teaching the Daily Mathematics Lesson to Children with Severe or Profound and Multiple Learning Difficulties (January 2003)
Ref: DfES 0033-2003 (Video); DfES 0032-2003 (File)

Medium Term Planning for Special Settings (July 2004)
Ref: DfES 0534-2004

Learning and Teaching for Dyslexic Children (May 2005)
Ref: DfES 1184-2005CDI

The above documents provide guidance and additional references to resources to support pupils.

5. Mental calculation

Introduction

The approach to calculation within the primary school has undergone radical change in recent years. This reflects an attempt to improve attainment in mathematics through the delay of written calculation, and greater emphasis on mental calculation. It is recognised that the early introduction of standard written methods can deny learners the opportunity to develop sufficient understanding of number and the number system. Instead, heavy reliance is placed on recall of rules and procedures.

The changes to the curriculum are significant and it is important that as a TA you have a secure understanding of the new methods and strategies used. They are different from the methods you were taught to calculate when at school and they require you to approach and think about mathematics in a different way. You need to become familiar and confident in their use.

CHAPTER OBJECTIVES

By the end of this chapter you should:

- understand the nature and role of mental calculation within the curriculum
- understand the strategies and methods used in mental calculation and feel confident in their use
- understand how you, as a TA, can support pupils' development of mental calculation skills.

What is mental calculation?

With the recent increased emphasis on mental calculation comes a redefinition. It is not simply instant recall of numerical facts or quick calculation without pencil and paper, although it may include both of these. At the heart of mental calculation lies the ability to work with number in a flexible manner; making decisions based on reasoning and a secure understanding of the number system. The teaching of mental calculation should not only have an impact also on knowledge and skills but also on pupils' attitude to mathematics. A child who is able to tackle a problem by selecting and using their own strategies demonstrates confidence and an understanding of the underlying structure of the mathematics involved. You can act as a good role model through your own attitude towards mental mathematics and a willingness to share the strategies you use with pupils.

Developing mental calculation strategies

The NNS Framework lists specific mental calculation strategies from Year 1. These are developed and added to for successive year groups. It is important as a TA that you are aware of all of these strategies so that you are able to recognise them when working with pupils. You may also play a role in assessing strategies that individual pupils are using and providing feedback to the teacher. Together you can then make a judgement as to what the next step is, to ensure progression and the development of efficiency in mental calculation. Key strategies will be explored in turn with suggestions of how you can support their development. For a full list and age-related expectations, please see the NNS Framework and the QCA booklet *Teaching Mental Calculation Strategies* (1999).

Counting on

One of the earliest mental strategies is counting on for addition. This strategy can be developed from the Reception year. Initially for addition, pupils will count out the quantities involved. In the calculation 5 + 2, first a group of five objects is counted out, followed by a group of two. Then all the objects are counted again to arrive at an answer. A counting-on strategy involves counting on the second number from the first. In the example of 5 + 2, the calculation is performed by holding a mental image of 5 and then counting on two while saying the number names, 'six, seven', possibly using fingers or a number line. If you have experience of working in Key Stage 1 you will be aware that for some children this strategy takes a long time to develop. However, it is worth persevering as it represents a significant step in the development of mental calculation strategies. It also makes the addition, easier to perform and less subject to error. When working with pupils who are counting out groups of objects for addition, encourage them to count on by covering up one group of objects, so that they can no longer count this group and are instead encouraged to count on. Success in this strategy should be reported to the teacher, who may then suggest the withdrawal of objects for counting and the use of an alternative resource such as a number line or fingers, for the purpose of counting on.

Using known facts to work out unknown facts

Knowledge of number facts can be used as a strategy to work out unknown facts; for example:

$72 + 30 = 102$ since $70 + 30 = 100$ (as $7 + 3 = 10$) and $100 + 2 = 102$

In this example the known fact is $7 + 3 = 10$. This fact used in conjunction with an understanding of place value allows the calculation to be completed successfully.

It has been traditional to learn *tables* and these were probably drilled into you when you were at school. Knowledge of tables still plays an important role, alongside other number facts. The NNS Framework includes a list of facts to be memorised for each year group. By Year 6 the expectation is that pupils will have a large bank of known facts at their disposal, including addition, subtraction, multiplication and division facts, halves and doubles.

As a TA you can support pupils in learning number facts by making resources and games which can be used in the classroom and taken home to provide practice and aid memorisation. This is discussed in Chapter 3.

For multiplication and division, helping pupils to group facts into *families* should aid memorisation and understanding of the relationships between them; for example.

$$3 \times 4 = 12$$
$$4 \times 3 = 12$$
$$12 \div 3 = 4$$
$$12 \div 4 = 3$$

Visual images can also help children to see connections and understand relationships. The use of an array is explored in Chapter 3.

Addition and subtraction of 9 or 11

This strategy is introduced in Key Stage 1, often using a 100 square (as discussed in Chapter 3). It requires adding 10 and then adjusting by 1.

Examples:

$12 + 11 = 12 + 10 + 1 = 23$
$12 + 9 = 12 + 10 - 1 = 21$

If pupils are struggling with the strategy using a 100 square, try using a number line as an alternative resource:

$12 + 9 = 12 + 10 - 1 = 21$

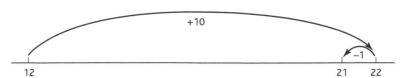

12   21   22

A number line can clarify whether the adjustment of 1 is a move forward or a move back along the number line. In the above example of adding 9 to 12, pupils reason that having added 10, they have gone too far along the number line and need to move one space back.

Using counting on for subtraction

In the early stages subtraction is performed by counting back. An easier strategy may to count on or forwards, finding the difference between the two numbers involved. Some children, however, do not feel confident in this strategy as they associate counting up with addition and do not understand why it works for subtraction. Below is a suggested strategy that links finding the difference with take away.

Example: 22 subtract 17

1. Using a number line, ask the pupil to find 22. Through discussion support the pupil in appreciating that 22 is not just a point on a number line (the ordinal aspect) but also the whole of the number line from 0 to 22 (the quantity aspect).

2. Ask the pupil to find 17. Again support the pupil in appreciating the quantity aspect of 17 as represented on the number line.

3. Remind pupils that the calculation requires them to take away 17 from 22. Ask them to represent the subtraction of 17 by scribbling out this part of the number line, as illustrated below. An alternative strategy is to place 22 counters above the number line at the start of the activity. The first 17 counters can then be taken away without counting, by using the 17 on the number line as a guide.

4. Ask the pupil what they need to do next to find how many are left. By this stage in the calculation it is usually obvious to pupils what the next stage is. Counting up from 17 to 22 will give them the answer. The act of scribbling out part of the number line is not a necessary part of the calculation, but it does give the pupil the security that 17 has been 'taken away' and helps to make sense of why counting up from 17 will produce the answer. You need to allow pupils to perform this act for a period of time, to develop confidence in the use of the strategy.

Using place value and partitioning

Several mental strategies involve the need to partition numbers. Partitioning requires splitting a number into parts, for example 24 is split into 20 and 4. This facilitates the strategy of adding the 20 first and then the 4 in an addition calculation. Place value involves an understanding that the value of a number is determined by the position the digits are placed in. When working with pupils make the distinction between the words 'digit' and 'number'. A digit only has a value when it has a place in a number, hence the term 'place value'. Consider the digit 2 as an example; on its own it is assumed to be in the units (ones) position and so has a value of two. However, if it is placed in the number 24 it no longer has a value of two but has taken on the value of 20 since it is now in the position to the left of four, the tens position. The use of resources to develop understanding of place value has been explored in Chapter 3. It is also illustrated in Chapter 7 in the context of decimals and the use of a place value grid.

Using partitioning and bridging through for addition

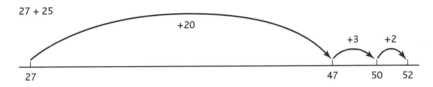

This method uses both the strategies of partitioning and bridging through:

1. Partition the 25 into 20 and 5. Notice the 27 is not partitioned. There is no need to partition both numbers
2. The 20 is added to the 27.
3. The 5 is then further partitioned into 3 and 2. The reason for this is to use the multiple of ten as a stepping stone. This is known as bridging through and can also be applied to hundreds and thousands.
4. Add the 3 to reach 50, using knowledge of number facts (7+3=10)
5. Now add the remaining 2 to reach 52. Adding on from a multiple of ten, in this case 50, should be an easy step.

This strategy at various levels of difficulty can be used from Year 2 onwards.

When working with pupils who are attempting to use this strategy there are several questions you need to ask:

- Are pupils able to make a jump of 20? If not, then encourage them to make two jumps of 10. If they are unable to count on in tens then discuss with the teacher the possible need for further work in this area.
- Are pupils able to partition 5 into 3 and 2? If not, then they need additional opportunities to learn number bonds. Perhaps you could make a card game as discussed in Chapter 3 which could be taken home for practice.

- Do pupils require a number line? The number line is not essential, but it is a helpful visual image and enables pupils to keep track of where they are in the calculation. If pupils are not ready to sketch their own number lines then write-on/wipe-off number lines which include all numbers are useful.

Partitioning for multiplication

The grid method for multiplication is explored in Chapter 6 and requires the need to partition numbers into hundreds, tens and units. It is sometimes helpful to partition numbers in other ways. The calculation 7×6 can be partitioned into $(5 \times 6) + (2 \times 6)$. This can be illustrated in the partitioning of a seven-by-six array.

Use the inverse relationship

The inverse relationship can be used as a mental strategy for both addition and subtraction, and multiplication and division. Known addition and multiplication facts can be used to calculate the related subtraction and division facts.

For example:

| If | $17 + 3 = 20$ | | If | $3 \times 5 = 15$ |
| Then | $20 - 3 = 17$ | | Then | $15 \div 5 = 3$ |

When working with pupils, alert them to facts that they already know and help them to make the connection to related facts.

The role of estimation in mental calculation

An estimation is not a wild guess but an intelligent consideration of the size of a number, based on reasoning from information already known. When working with pupils on calculation you should encourage them to estimate before they calculate. The advantage of this is that it encourages pupils to focus on the size of the numbers involved and to consider possible strategies. For younger children you might simplify the process using the concept of more or less. You could ask 'do you think the answer will be more or less than 10?' The language of more than or less than is useful here as it avoids the learner having to give an exact answer. Many pupils mistakenly assume that the answers in mathematics always need to be precise, and have been observed changing their estimate once the exact number has been revealed!

Another useful strategy is to encourage pupils to estimate within a range, for example: $67 + 91$ is more than 100 but less than 200 since both numbers are less than 100 but 91 is close to 100. This gives pupils the opportunity to think about the calculation and the numbers involved. You could also use a number line as a resource, where pupils mark on their range. This enables them to see with greater clarity if their answer is within the range. You should encourage Key Stage 2 pupils to use known number facts to assist estimation. For example, 139 divided by 9 is more than 10 but less than 20 since ten nines are 90 and 20 nines are 180. Estimation is also a useful checking strategy after the calculation has been completed. Is the answer close to the estimate? If the answer is yes then it is probably correct, if not it is likely that an error has been made.

Does mental calculation involve writing?

Mental calculation does involve writing. This may seem like a contradiction; however, it is unreasonable to expect all mental calculation to be carried out without some form of jottings. The use of informal jottings can support calculation strategies and enable pupils to experience achievement rather than failure. You may need to support pupils in the development of informal jottings. An example is given below for doubling 36.

Mentally the 36 is partitioned into 30 and 6.

Jot down double 30	60
Jot down double 6	12
Add together	72

The jotting down of interim numbers frees up the mind to think about the calculation. Mental calculation is still taking place as mental strategies are being employed to tackle the calculation. When you are working with pupils either in an oral and mental starter or in group work, encourage them to make use of jottings. This may be through modelling your own use of jottings for mental calculation. Sometimes a small whiteboard for jotting is valuable as pupils feel more confident if the jottings can be erased.

Does the teaching of mental calculation necessarily develop understanding?

The aim in teaching mental calculation is not just to develop strategies but also to develop a secure understanding of number. However, this does not always happen and it is important that when working with pupils you check that they understand the methods they are using. If you discover that they do not understand then you need to discuss this with the teacher and together you can decide on strategies for developing understanding. The case study below illustrates this point.

Case study

Teacher: Yesterday we learnt to add ten, using a 100 square. Can anyone suggest how we add 9?
Annie: You move down one and then back one.
Teacher: Yes, that's right, so what is 22 + 9? (*pointing to 22 on the 100 square*)
Brian: 31
Teacher: That's right, well done. Can anyone tell me what 44 + 9 is?
Cathy: 55
Teacher: Not quite, you have moved the wrong way (*outlines the movement using the 100 square*). You need to move down one and back one.

The teacher asks for 53 + 9 and 42 + 9; each receive a correct response. She models the movement each time.
Teacher: Now can anyone tell me how we might add 11?
Annie: You move down one and forward one.
Teacher: Yes that's right, so what's 21 + 11?
Daniel: 32
Teacher: Yes that's right, how did you do it?
Daniel: I moved down one and along one.

Further examples were explored in the same manner.

The children were then given several calculations to complete, using a 100 square. The teaching assistant Paula worked with Daniel and was confident of his success as he had answered a question correctly in the whole-class session. She checked he had the first question correct and then left him to work independently for a while. When she returned she realised that several of his answers were incorrect. She questioned him:

Paula : Can you tell me how you worked out the answer for 22 + 9?
Daniel: I found 22 on my hundred square and then moved down one and along one and got to 33.

Paula: Why did you move forward one and not back one?
Daniel: I don't know, that's the bit I keep forgetting, I'm not sure if I should move forward or back.

Reflection on the case study
Daniel was confused as to whether adding 9 necessitated a forward or backward move on the 100 square and there was similar confusion regarding the addition of 11. It transpired that Daniel had not understood why the procedure worked and was therefore just following the rule, which he sometimes forgot. Paula reported this to the teacher, who addressed the problem in the next lesson.

PRACTICAL TASK

The aim of this task is for you to explore mental calculation strategies and the use of a number line to illustrate your thinking.

Consider the strategies that could be used for the following calculations. Attempt to illustrate each one, using a number line.

a. 36 + 21   b. 24 + 23   c. 97 + 19   d. 87 − 69   e. 13 × 12   f. 98 ÷ 7

Answers and reflection

The following answers are only suggestions. There is no one correct strategy for any calculation. Strategies are often a personal preference; however, you need to consider both for yourself and the pupils you work with whether the strategy used for a particular calculation could be more efficient.

a. 36 + 21 using partitioning   36 + 20 + 1 = 57

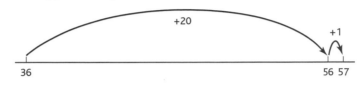

b. 24 + 23 using near doubles   24 + 24 − 1 = 47

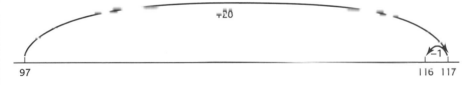

This strategy has not been discussed in this chapter but is in the NNS Framework. Doubles are expected to be memorised and then used to calculate near doubles. Double 24 is used and then adjusted by 1. You may have used partitioning as in example a.

c. 97 + 19 using a near multiple of 10   97 + 20 − 1 = 116

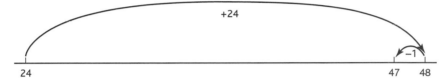

This is the same strategy as adding 9, which has already been discussed. The jump of 20 can be completed in two jumps of 10.

d. 87 − 69 is calculated using a counting up strategy and finding the difference between 69 and 87.   1 + 10 + 7 = 18

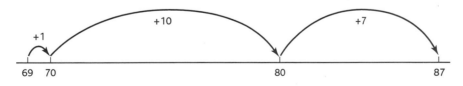

Do not forget that when working with pupils it is sometimes useful to include the part of the number line from 0 to 69 and scribble this out to represent taking away.

e. 13 × 12 using partitioning   (10 × 12) + (3 × 12) = 156

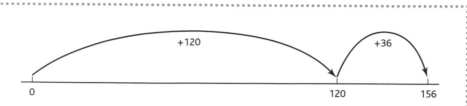

Generally this type of calculation is recorded in a grid. This is discussed in Chapter 6.

f.   98 ÷ 7 = (10 groups of 7) + (4 groups of 7) = 14 groups of 7

This strategy is discussed in greater detail in Chapter 6. The question is interpreted as 'how many groups of 7 are in 98?' The answer is calculated by counting up the number of groups on a number line.

In the tasks above you were asked to illustrate your strategies on a number line. Although a number line is not always used when calculating mentally, it is useful as an illustration to explain a strategy to a pupil or for a pupil to explain a strategy to you.

Summary

In this chapter we have explored mental calculation and the development of calculation strategies. As a TA you need to:

- understand the range of strategies used in your school and illustrated in the NNS Framework
- explain and illustrate a strategy to a pupil who needs support
- check that pupils understand the strategies they are using.

References and resources

MathsWeb, Leicestershire's numeracy website, www.leics.org.uk, has printable resources and games to support mental calculation.

Crossbow Education website, www.crossboweducation.com, specialises in games for children with difficulties in reading, spelling and memory and produces game activities for literacy and numeracy. 'Oh No' is a times-table photocopiable game book.

DfES (1999) *The National Numeracy Strategy Framework for Teaching Mathematics.* London: DfES

QCA (1999) *The National Numeracy Strategy, Teaching Mental Calculation Strategies.* London: QCA

6. Written calculation

Introduction

With the increased emphasis on mental calculation comes a repositioning of the role of written calculation. Standard written calculation is delayed in the NNS Framework until Year 3, where it may begin if children have developed an appropriate grasp of mental calculation. Its development then continues through to Year 6. The distinction between written and mental calculation is not as clear as it once was. In this chapter we shall define standard written calculation as traditional column methods, many of which you are probably familiar with from your own school days.

$$\begin{array}{r} 1\ \ 2\ \ 3 \\ +\ \ 2\ \ 4\ \ 9 \\ \hline \end{array} \qquad \begin{array}{r} 6\ \ 4\ \ 2 \\ -\ \ 4\ \ 5\ \ 9 \\ \hline \end{array} \qquad \begin{array}{r} 2\ \ 4\ \ 6 \\ \times\ \ \ \ 5\ \ 7 \\ \hline \end{array} \qquad 27\overline{\smash{\big)}\,249}$$

It is important that when moving from a mental to a more formal method of calculation, this is handled in such a way as to maintain an understanding of the mathematics. Mental calculation and its development continue to play a key role even after standard written methods have been introduced.

The approach to calculation will be different in individual schools and even for different pupils. It may be that you are involved, alongside the teacher, in deciding which approach to take for an individual or group of pupils. In order to support pupils effectively in their learning you need not only to be familiar with the methods used, but also understand the reasoning behind their use. This will be considered as we look at the four operations of addition, subtraction, multiplication and division.

HLTA STANDARDS

2.1   They have sufficient understanding of their specialist area to support pupils' learning, and are able to acquire further knowledge to contribute effectively and with confidence to the classes in which they are involved.

2.2   They are familiar with the school curriculum, the age-related expectations of pupils, the main teaching methods and the testing/examination frameworks in the subjects and age ranges in which they are involved.

2.3   They understand the aims, content, teaching strategies and intended outcomes for the lessons in which they are involved, and understand the place of these in the related teaching programme.

By the end of this chapter you should:

- understand the meaning and purpose of a standard written method for addition, subtraction, multiplication and division
- understand the link between mental and written calculation
- understand how to move from mental to written calculation while maintaining understanding of the mathematics involved.

Addition

Typical standard written methods for addition require the addition of the units first. However, when operating mentally, it is generally preferable to add the most significant digit first. The most significant digit is that representing the largest part of the number; so 54 + 22 can be calculated as $(50 + 20) + (4 + 2)$; with the most significant digits added first.

```
123 + 156 is written as:
    123
+   156
    ────
    200
     70
      9
    ────
    279
```

Many schools make use of the informal (expanded) written method, presented in the NNS Framework to ease the transition from mental to a standard written method.

Here the calculation is written vertically as in the standard written method. The most significant digits are added first, in this case the hundreds, and recorded in full, then the tens and the ones. The advantage of this method is that the learner is made to think of the value of each digit involved in the calculation and can work with understanding. Also, by adding the most significant digits first, a link is made to mental calculation. The final stage of the calculation is simply a combining of the number 200 and 70 and 9 as 279. Progression can then be made to adding from the right with the least significant digits added first.

```
    123
+   156
    ────
      9
     70
    200
    ────
    279
```

This in turn leads to the standard written method which you will be familiar with.

The final stage of the process involving the traditional compact written method can be a significant leap for some children to achieve with secure understanding and this should not be rushed. If it is introduced and pupils are making errors (as illustrated in the case study below) then they need to return to an informal or a mental method.

Case study

Tim was working with a group of Year 4 pupils during the daily mathematics lesson. The children had been introduced to a compact standard written method for addition and had been given some calculations to complete. Tim observed that all the pupils in the group had got the first three calculations correct and concluded that they had understood the method and very little intervention on his part would be required. However, on completion of the fourth calculation he realised that he was mistaken in his initial assessment.

```
  1 2 4        1 3 1        2 4 3        2 3 6
+1 2 2       +1 4 3       +1 2 2       +1 2 5
───────      ───────      ───────      ───────
  2 4 6        2 7 4        3 6 5      3 5 1 1
───────      ───────      ───────      ───────
```

Most of the children in the group had got the fourth calculation incorrect (see above). He stopped the group and copied the calculation, including the incorrect answer onto a small whiteboard.

Tim: Are you happy with the answer?
Child 1: Yes because 2 and 1 make 3, 3 and 2 make 5 and 5 and 6 make 11.
Tim: What is the answer then?
Child 2: Three hundred and 50, um 1 or 11 maybe?

Tim helped the children read the number as 'three thousand, five hundred and eleven'.

Tim: If we are adding 100 and something and one hundred and something; is the answer going to be 3,000?

With support the pupils realised that the answer could not possibly be 3,511. Tim went through the method again, reminding the pupils to start from the right and that it was only in the final column they were adding ones or units; the other two columns represented tens and hundreds. However, they still seemed insecure. On discussion with the teacher afterwards it was decided that these pupils needed to return to recording their answers using an informal expanded method.

Reflection on the case study

Moving to the next stage in mathematics is obviously important; however, this should only take place when understanding is secure and pupils have developed the necessary skills. The pupils in this case study had been moved to the next stage of a standard written method, but then needed to return to a more informal method as it was revealed their understanding was not as secure as it first appeared. Whether to return a pupil to an earlier stage or persevere with age-related objectives is often a difficult decision to make. As a TA, working closely with a pupil you may be able to monitor and provide feedback to the teacher to support this decision.

Subtraction

The standard written method of decomposition for
subtraction has often caused difficulty for pupils.
Decomposition involves 'borrowing' from the digit to the
left when the value of the digit on top is less than that
underneath, as illustrated at the beginning of this chapter.
The NNS Framework does suggest a method. This involves
partitioning of the numbers, so 786 – 254 becomes:

$$
\begin{array}{r}
700 + 80 + 6 \\
- \ 200 + 50 + 4 \\
\hline
500 + 30 + 2
\end{array}
$$

The above example is fairly straightforward; the
difficulty arises when one or more of the parts on the
top row are smaller than those, located directly
underneath, as in 434 – 316.

$$
\begin{array}{r}
400 + 30 + 4 \\
- \ 300 + 10 + 6 \\
\hline
\end{array}
$$

Six, in the units column cannot be subtracted from four
and leave a positive result. The top number needs to be
repartitioned.

$$
\begin{array}{r}
400 + 20 + 14 \\
- \ 300 + 10 + \ 6 \\
\hline
100 + 10 + \ 8 \\
\hline
= 118
\end{array}
$$

This then leads to the standard compact method of
decomposition; however, this is still a significant step.

$$
\begin{array}{ccc}
4 & {}^2\cancel{3}\,{}^1 4 \\
3 & 1 & 6 \\
\hline
1 & 1 & 8 \\
\hline
\end{array}
$$

Many pupils continue to make errors in the complex procedure of crossing out
numbers and writing smaller ones. Many also lose sight of the place value and do
not fully appreciate that the one carried across from the middle column is not a one,
but a ten, which is why the number in the units column then becomes 14 (10 + 4).

Two alternative methods have been adopted by some schools that are worth
considering.

Negative number subtraction

In the above example there was the need to repartition the numbers, since we
cannot take 6 from 4. However, this is not entirely accurate: we can take 6
from 4; the answer is –2.

So the above calculation could be written:

$$
\begin{array}{rrr}
400 & 30 & 4 \\
300 & 10 & 6 \\
\hline
100 & 20 & -2
\end{array}
\quad = 118\ (100 + 20 + -2)
$$

This method is not referenced in the NNS Framework, but has been adopted
by some schools and included in their mathematics policy.

Counting up for subtraction

This is strictly speaking a mental strategy and is discussed in the previous chapter. However, even when handling large and difficult numbers, efficiency in its use can be developed.

327 − 186 = 4 + 10 + 127 = 141

Some formalise this strategy into a vertical presentation.

	3	2	7	
− 1	8	6		
	4	to	190	
	1 0	to	200	
	1 2 7	to	327	

However, it is questionable whether the vertical presentation advances the compactness or efficiency of the strategy. For many children the visual image of the number line is valuable in keeping track of the calculation.

Multiplication

Most primary teachers have found the grid method of multiplication (as illustrated in the NNS Framework) a successful strategy and in fact many do not see the need for moving pupils into the traditional standard written method. Although it is recorded in a standard format, it uses mental strategies for calculation.

The following is a suggested progression, building on pupils' understanding of arrays from Year 2 and maintaining understanding of the place value involved.

1.   The array for the multiplication is presented, in this case 12 × 4

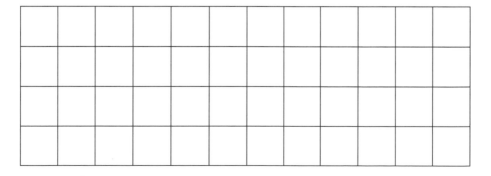

The rows of 12 are then partitioned into 10 and 2:

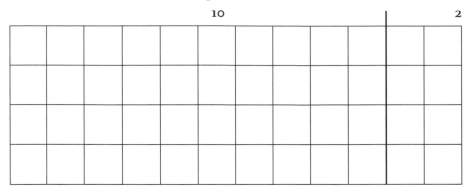

There are now four rows of 10 and four rows of two

4 rows of 10 (4×10) = 40

4 rows of 2 (4×2) = 8

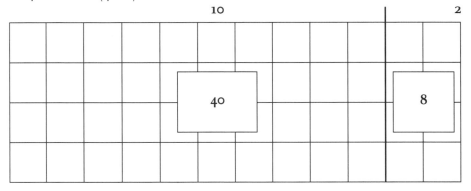

Each part of the array is multiplied out separately and then the two parts added together, so the answer is 40 + 8 = 48.

The next stage is to remove the squares, so the grid is a representation of 12×4 rather than the actual number of squares for 12×4. This may initially be represented using fairly accurate proportions, so the 4×10 portion is larger than the 4×2 portion:

```
        10      2
      ┌──────┬─────┐
  4   │  40  │  8  │
      └──────┴─────┘
```

40 + 8 = 48

The array can then be presented, using a divided rectangle (not to scale).

```
       10    2
      ┌────┬────┐
  4   │ 40 │ 8  │
      └────┴────┘
```

This method can then be extended to two by two digit calculations and then three digit calculations.

24×321

	300	20	1
20	6000	400	20
4	1200	80	4

$$6420$$
$$+1284$$
$$\overline{7704}$$

It should be noted that the progression outlined above should be developed over time as understanding is developed and secured. The advantage of the grid method is that the language pupils use to calculate helps to maintain an understanding of the value of each part of the number; so that '4 times 300 is 1,200' instead of '4 times 3 is 12' (as is often the case in the standard written method).

Errors made using the standard written method sometimes occur because children move into a procedural mode, consequently bypassing the need to consider the size of the numbers involved. They may miss out a stage such as moving one space to the left when multiplying by ten and writing a zero in as a place holder in the units position. Where the formal standard method is introduced it should be taught with understanding, making links to the grid method.

Division

As with multiplication, there have been significant changes in methods used for division. Chunking (or multiple subtraction) is introduced in the NNS Framework to bridge the gap between mental and written calculation.

PRACTICAL TASK

The aim of this practical task is for you to consider how you would explain the following calculation to a pupil who was having difficulty understanding.

13 $\overline{)274}$

Reflection on the task

First of all you probably said, '13 into 2 doesn't go'. If you think about it, it does go because the 2 is not in fact 2 but 200. You then probably said, '13 into 27 goes 2 times with one remaining'. This again doesn't make sense since the number is not 27 but 270. This method does not lend itself to the development of understanding. This is the reasoning behind using the chunking method; it is easier to for pupils to explain and understand.

The chunking method for this calculation will be explored in two formats, on a number line and vertically.

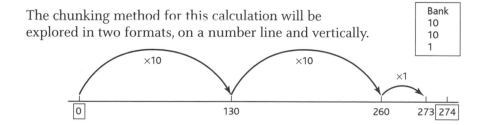

The language accompanying the method is important:

How many groups of 13 are there in 274?

If we count them up in groups we can calculate how many. Counting in multiples of ten is a useful strategy as most pupils find ten easier to handle than other multiples.

There are ten 13s in 130.

Another ten 13s gets us to 260.

One more 13 gets us to 273 and there is 1 left over, so the answer is 10 + 10 + 1 groups of 13 in 274, and one left over.

This equals 21 remainder 1

Notice the *bank* in the top right-hand corner. This may be useful in keeping track of the number of 13s calculated. Every time a group of 13 is jumped, it is recorded in the bank.

Written vertically it would be:

$$
\begin{array}{r}
2\ 7\ 4 \\
-\ 1\ 3\ 0\ (10 \times 13) \\
\hline
1\ 4\ 4 \\
-\ 1\ 3\ 0\ (10 \times 13) \\
\hline
1\ 4 \\
-\quad 1\ 3\ (1 \times 13) \\
\hline
1 \\
\hline
\end{array}
$$

= 21 r 1

As can be seen, the two methods of chunking are similar: both require subtraction of groups of 13 from 274. However, the method of subtraction is slightly different. In the number line example the subtraction is achieved by counting up the number of groups of 13 to reach 274. In the vertical example the groups of 13 are removed, or counted back from 274 to zero.

The NNS Framework illustrates the vertical method but not the number line method. If pupils have been introduced to the vertical method and a pupil you are supporting is having difficulty, you may discuss with the teacher using the number line method, particularly if the pupil is confident in counting up for subtraction.

Reflection

In this chapter we have explored a variety of methods of calculation; there may be others that exist in your school. The more recent informal methods have been introduced by the Numeracy Strategy to bridge the gap between mental and written calculation and to move from one to the other with understanding. It is important that you are not only familiar with these, but that you understand how they work and the reasoning behind their use. Unlike mental calculation, pupils' do not need a range of written methods; one efficient written method is sufficient. If one method is not working for a pupil, you should discuss this with the teacher and together you may decide to try an alternative method. Your monitoring of a pupils' response should provide valuable information which the teacher can then use to inform future planning.

The role of the standard written method is not as significant as it once was, due to the increased emphasis on mental calculation. Mental methods should still be developed and used even after standard written methods have been introduced. Pupils then need to learn to make decisions about the most appropriate method for a given calculation. You may be able to support them in making those decisions.

Summary

- Bridging the gap between mental and standard written calculation and ensuring secure understanding is crucial for successful progression.
- Pupils should be supported in developing the ability to make decisions about the most appropriate method for a given calculation.
- You need to ensure that you are familiar and confident in the use of the methods used in the classrooms you work in. This may require asking for information and practising with examples, before working with pupils. Both the NNS Framework and the QCA booklet *Teaching Written Calculation* will be useful documents.

References

DfES (1999) *The National Numeracy Strategy Framework for Teaching Mathematics*. London: DfES

QCA (1999) *The National Numeracy Strategy, Teaching Written Calculation Strategies*. Suffolk: QCA

7. Fractions, decimals, percentages, ratio and proportion

Introduction

Fractions, decimals, percentages, ratio and proportion are traditionally areas of mathematics which many children find difficult. There is a variety of reasons for this. In this chapter we shall explore some of those reasons and also seek to develop your own knowledge and understanding in this area in order that you may support children more effectively in their learning.

HLTA STANDARDS

2.1 They have sufficient understanding of their specialist area to support pupils' learning, and are able to acquire further knowledge to contribute effectively and with confidence to the classes in which they are involved.

2.2 They are familiar with the school curriculum, the age-related expectations of pupils, the main teaching methods and the testing/examination frameworks in the subjects and age ranges in which they are involved.

2.3 They understand the aims, content, teaching strategies and intended outcomes for the lessons in which they are involved and understand the place of these in the related teaching programme.

CHAPTER OBJECTIVES

By the end of this chapter you should:

● understand the main aims of the curriculum with regard to fractions, decimals, percentages, ratio and proportion

● understand the meaning and nature of fractions, decimals, percentages, ratio and proportion and the relationship between them

● understand the importance of equivalence within mathematics

● understand the importance of making connections within mathematics

● develop the use of strategies and resources to support learning in this area.

Fractions, decimals, percentages, ratio and proportion within the primary curriculum

Within the NNS Framework, fractions and in particular the concept of a half are mentioned as early as Reception; although they are more formally introduced in Year 2 in the context of halves and quarters of quantities and shapes. Other fractions are introduced in Year 3 where the concept of equivalent fractions begins to be developed. Decimals are introduced in Year 2, in the context of money, and further developed in Year 4, making connections to pupils' understanding of fractions. Percentages, ratio and proportion are introduced in Year 5 and further developed in Year 6.

Fractions

There are two main reasons why fractions cause particular difficulties for learners. Firstly, a fraction can be viewed in different ways and model a variety of different contexts. Secondly, fractions are expressed using different denominators (the bottom part of the fraction), which make them difficult to compare and calculate with. Two fractions may look different when in fact they are the same; for example $\frac{1}{2}$ and $\frac{2}{4}$.

Fractions model a variety of different contexts:

- A part of a whole; for example, where $\frac{1}{3}$ represents one part of a whole that has been divided into three equal parts.
- A part of a quantity; for example, where $\frac{4}{12}$ is viewed as 4 out of a group of 12.
- A position on a number line.
- A division calculation, so $\frac{3}{4}$ is 3 ÷ 4.

Context B

This context represents a *fraction as a division calculation*.

The calculation is 3 ÷ 4.

Three apples are divided equally among four people.

One way to do this is to cut each apple into four, in doing this multiples of four are created and so the apple can be shared equally among four people. Each piece of apple represents $\frac{1}{4}$ and each person receives three of those quarters $(\frac{3}{4})$.

Both contexts, although they may appear different, are represented by the fraction $\frac{3}{4}$. It is important when working with pupils that they are exposed to a variety of different, contexts and that their understanding of fractions is not limited to one model. Pupils usually begin by exploring fractions in the context of shapes divided into equal parts. This is a useful starting point, but their understanding of fractions should not be limited to this example.

Fractions are expressed using different denominators

Unlike whole numbers, decimals or percentages, fractions are expressed using different denominators. These often need to be converted to the same denominator for ease of comparison and calculation. This makes them more difficult than other numbers to work with, as a comparison with decimals and percentages illustrates.

Decimals are always expressed in the same format: that of tenths, hundredths and thousandths etc. Making a comparison between 0.3 add 0.4 is relatively straightforward. A comparison between $\frac{1}{3}$ and $\frac{2}{5}$ may require a little more thinking.

Percentages are always expressed in hundredths. This common format lends itself to ease of comparison. We know instantly that 73% of a quantity is less than 86% of the same quantity, whereas identifying the larger fraction from $\frac{8}{11}$ and $\frac{6}{7}$ is more difficult.

PRACTICAL TASK

The aim of this task is for you to consider some of the misconceptions that pupils can have in this area and how you can address these and develop understanding.

Consider why pupils may develop the following misconceptions and suggest strategies for developing understanding:

a. $\frac{1}{9}$ is greater than $\frac{1}{8}$

b. 0.09 is greater than 0.1

c. a percentage cannot be more than 100.

Reflection on the task

a. $\frac{1}{9}$ is greater than $\frac{1}{8}$

It is easy to see why pupils may think in this way. They consider $\frac{1}{9}$ as greater than $\frac{1}{8}$ since 9 is greater than 8. A resource known as a fraction wall can help to show that $\frac{1}{9}$ is in fact less than $\frac{1}{8}$:

1									
$\frac{1}{2}$					$\frac{1}{2}$				
$\frac{1}{3}$			$\frac{1}{3}$			$\frac{1}{3}$			
$\frac{1}{4}$		$\frac{1}{4}$		$\frac{1}{4}$			$\frac{1}{4}$		
$\frac{1}{5}$		$\frac{1}{5}$		$\frac{1}{5}$		$\frac{1}{5}$		$\frac{1}{5}$	
$\frac{1}{6}$		$\frac{1}{6}$		$\frac{1}{6}$		$\frac{1}{6}$		$\frac{1}{6}$	$\frac{1}{6}$
$\frac{1}{7}$		$\frac{1}{7}$	$\frac{1}{7}$		$\frac{1}{7}$		$\frac{1}{7}$		$\frac{1}{7}$
$\frac{1}{8}$	$\frac{1}{8}$	$\frac{1}{8}$	$\frac{1}{8}$	$\frac{1}{8}$	$\frac{1}{8}$	$\frac{1}{8}$	$\frac{1}{8}$		
$\frac{1}{9}$	$\frac{1}{9}$	$\frac{1}{9}$	$\frac{1}{9}$	$\frac{1}{9}$	$\frac{1}{9}$	$\frac{1}{9}$	$\frac{1}{9}$	$\frac{1}{9}$	
$\frac{1}{10}$	$\frac{1}{10}$	$\frac{1}{10}$	$\frac{1}{10}$	$\frac{1}{10}$	$\frac{1}{10}$	$\frac{1}{10}$	$\frac{1}{10}$	$\frac{1}{10}$	$\frac{1}{10}$

b. 0.09 is greater than 0.1

Again pupils generalise without considering all of the information. They see the digits 9 and 1 and conclude that since the number nine is larger than the number one, 0.09 must be greater than 0.1. The distinction between the word digit and the word number, as discussed in Chapter 5, is important in this context. The digit nine does not represent the number 9 since it has not been placed in the units (ones) position, but has instead been placed in the hundredths position. It thus represents 9 hundredths, which can also be expressed as the fraction 9/100. Likewise, the digit one has not been placed in the unit (ones) position, but has been placed in the tenths position and represents 1 tenth or $\frac{1}{10}$.

This example requires exploration of place value in terms of looking at the value of each digit in the numbers involved. A place value grid is a useful resource:

Hundreds	Tens	Units (ones)	Tenths	Hundredths
		0	1	
		0	0	9

Once pupils have reached a certain stage in their learning they readily understand that tens are smaller than hundreds and units are smaller than tens. This understanding needs to be applied to decimals. Tenths are smaller than units and hundredths are smaller than tenths. The value of the digits decreases as we move from left to right across the place value grid. The confusion may lie in the words used and some children reason that since hundreds are larger than tens, hundredths must be larger than tenths. The visual image of the place value grid and the positioning of the column headings may assist understanding. Additionally, concrete apparatus which demonstrate the size of a hundredth in comparison to a tenth may be valuable.

c. A percentage cannot be more than 100

In some contexts a percentage cannot be more than 100, such as a bag of sweets. 100% is all of the sweets. However, in terms of an increase where you receive a 110% pay rise; this is possible, although not likely! It is important that children not only know but understand why they are incorrect when they say a percentage cannot be more than 100. This can be done by exploring an appropriate example:

Child A has two sweets and child B has two sweets

If child B is then given two more sweets we can say that he has had a 100% increase or that he has 100% more than child A.

We can then ask if it is possible for child B to be given any more sweets. Of course the answer is yes. He will then have had an increase of more than 100%.

In each of the examples of the misconceptions discussed above there has been an attempt to explain and develop understanding with the support of resources. It is important that pupils' misconceptions are explored with them so that they can realise why their thinking is incorrect. It is insufficient to simply correct them without explanation. As a TA you may have the time to do this with an individual pupil. Your own knowledge and confidence will grow as you take the time first to clarify an aspect of mathematics in your own mind and then to explain it to a pupil. If you are unsure of an aspect of mathematics, do not be afraid to discuss this with the teacher. Alternatively, you can do your own research. Alongside this book two other books are recommended to support your own development of subject knowledge. These are referenced at the end of this chapter.

Making connections between fractions, decimals and percentages

It is important that pupils recognise the connections between fractions, decimals and percentages. $\frac{1}{2}$, 50% and 0.5 are equivalents. This means that in a bag of 12 sweets, $\frac{1}{2}$ of the bag is 6; 50% of it is 6; and 0.5 of it is 6. They represent the same proportion of the bag of sweets. Equivalence between apparently different sets of numbers is an important concept within mathematics. Understanding of the individual concepts of fractions, decimals and percentages will be strengthened by the recognition of equivalence.

PRACTICAL TASK

The aim of this task is to enable you to develop your own understanding of equivalence so you may more effectively support pupils.

- Draw three lines and mark on equivalent fractions, percentages and decimals, as below.

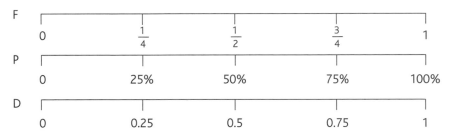

- Now add $\frac{1}{8}$ to the fraction line, and its equivalent on the percentage and decimal line ($\frac{1}{8}$ is half of a quarter, so to find the equivalent percentage, halve 25%).

  Have you noticed the relationship between the percentage and decimal line? The digits are the same. This is because a percentage is expressed as part of a hundred and a decimal is expressed as part of one. Thus taking the percentage as a whole number and dividing it by 100 will give the equivalent decimal.

- Now add the other eighths and their equivalent percentages and decimals. Notice you already have 2, 4 and 6 eighths as these are equivalent to $\frac{1}{4}$, $\frac{2}{4}$ (or $\frac{1}{2}$) and $\frac{3}{4}$.

- Repeat the activity with three new lines for tenths and their equivalent percentages and decimals. Also identify where the fifths would come on the fraction line.

- Repeat the activity for thirds.

Note the completed lines are shown at the end of the chapter.

Reflection on the activity

In this activity you were making key connections between fractions, decimals and percentages and recognising equivalence. It is worth memorising some key facts, such as $\frac{1}{5}$ is equivalent to 20% and 0.2. Once these have been memorised and the principles understood, then others can be quickly derived. You then have the option of converting between them, so if you are uncomfortable working with fractions, you can convert and work with decimals or percentages instead. These alternative strategies may be useful in supporting a pupil who is struggling in one area.

Other useful connections: a percentage web

Below is an example of a percentage web. The quantity in the centre is given and then pupils are asked to calculate percentages using reasoning and mental strategies.

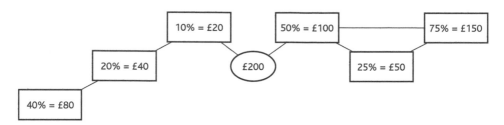

50% is equal to £100 and has been calculated by halving £200, which is 100%.

25% is equal to £50 and has been calculated by halving £100, which is equal to 50%.

75% is equal to £150 and has been calculated by adding 50% and 25%.

10% was calculated by dividing £200 by 10.

20% and 40% were then calculated by doubling 10%.

You may wish to complete the web by calculating other percentages. The advantage of this type of activity is that pupils are engaged in making connections and using their own mental strategies to calculate.

Ratio and proportion

Proportion compares part to whole and is therefore usually expressed in terms of a fraction, decimal or percentage. Ratio makes a different comparison and compares part to part. A comparison between ratio and proportion is illustrated in the following examples:

What proportion of the stick below is black?

The answer is 1 in 4, or $\frac{1}{4}$ or 25% or 0.25. All of these are equivalent

statements and express the proportion of the black segments in relation to the whole stick.

What is the ratio of black to white segments?

This question is not asking for a comparison between the whole and a part; but between two different parts of the stick; the black segments and the white segments. There is one black segment and three white segments so the ratio is 1 to 3 or 1:3.

Consider another example

What proportion of the stick is black?

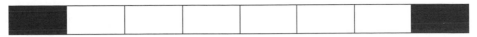

The answer is 2 in 8 or $\frac{2}{8}$ or $\frac{1}{4}$ (the equivalent of $\frac{2}{8}$) or 25% or 0.25.

What is the ratio of black to white segments?

The answer is 2 to 6 or 2:6, since there are two black segments and six white segments. This can also be expressed as 1 to 3 or 1:3. For every single black segment there are three white segments. Ratio is generally broken down and expressed in its simplest form using whole numbers.

Exploring the idea of equivalence in fractions and ratio

Equivalence has already been referred to in relation to fractions, decimals and percentages. It is an important concept and it is necessary to understand it as the same idea within any context it is applied to. We shall explore and develop understanding of the idea first within fractions, and then within ratio.

Equivalent fractions

All the fractions listed below are equivalent to $\frac{1}{2}$:

$\frac{2}{4}, \frac{3}{6}, \frac{4}{8}, \frac{5}{10}, \frac{6}{12}, \frac{7}{14}, \frac{8}{16}, \frac{9}{18}, \frac{10}{20}, \frac{60}{120}$

What makes them equivalent is:

a. The relationship between the top and bottom part of a fraction. The top number is half the bottom number, or we could say the bottom number is twice the top number. This relationship is the same for all the fractions listed.

b. The relationship between fractions when comparisons are made:

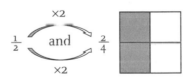

Both the top and bottom numbers have been multiplied by the same number, in this case 2. This action maintains the relationship and so the fractions are equivalent. The image of the array also illustrates this point. $\frac{1}{2}$ and $\frac{2}{4}$ can be viewed as representing the same area.

We shall illustrate this again by making the same comparison between another pair of fractions:

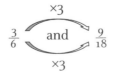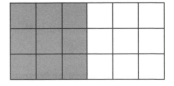

Here both the top and bottom numbers have been multiplied by 3. The same operation applied to both parts of the fraction maintains the relationship and hence the fractions are equivalent. We could also look at the relationship when moving the other way from $\frac{9}{18}$ to $\frac{3}{6}$. This time both the top and bottom numbers have been divided by 3. The image of the array shows that the part shaded is both $\frac{9}{18}$ and $\frac{3}{6}$. nine out of eighteen squares are shaded, hence $\frac{9}{18}$. Three out of six columns are shaded, hence $\frac{3}{6}$.

Any operation of multiplication or division applied to both the top and bottom parts of the fraction will maintain the relationship and produce equivalent fractions.

Note the top and bottom parts of the fraction are technically referred to as the numerator and denominator. These terms are introduced in Year 5.

Equivalent ratios

The idea of equivalence is the same when applied to ratio. Here are some equivalent ratios:

1	:	2
2	:	4
3	:	6
4	:	8
5	:	10
60	:	120

Here the same multiplicative relationship can be seen between individual parts of the ratio (in the above example the second number is always twice the first) and also between pairs of ratio. If we compare:

$$
\begin{array}{ccc}
& 1 & : & 2 \\
\times 5 & & & \times 5 \\
& 5 & : & 10
\end{array}
$$

When both sides of the ratio are multiplied or divided by the same number, an equivalent ratio is produced, in this case a multiplication of five.

This idea of equivalence in ratio is very useful for solving problems, as the following case study illustrates.

Case study

Shalini a teaching assistant was working with two Year 6 pupils who had been asked to paint the grass area of a large mural which depicted the school building and its grounds. Unfortunately there was no green paint available so the teacher had discussed with the pupils how they could mix blue and yellow paint to produce green paint. She told them that they would need more yellow paint than blue and suggested three scoops of yellow paint for every two scoops of blue paint. She then left the pupils with Shalini to support the completion of the task. Shalini reminded the pupils that they had been working on the topic of ratio in the mathematics lesson earlier that day. She then engaged them in a discussion relating to the ratio of blue to yellow paint.

Shalini: If we need two scoops of blue paint for every three scoops of yellow paint, what is the ratio of blue to yellow paint?
Ali: I know its two to three.
Shalini: yes that's right. I think we will need a lot of paint as we have a large area to cover. I think we will need eight scoops of blue paint. How much yellow paint will we need?
Ian and Ali looked blank.
Shalini: If we only used four scoops of blue paint, how much yellow paint would we need?
Ian: I know six.
Shalini asked Ian to explain how he had arrived at his answer.
Ian: Well we've added another two scoops of blue paint, which means that we need to add another three scoops of yellow paint.
Shalini: That's right because the ratio is two to three, which means that for every two scoops of blue paint we add, we need to add three scoops of yellow paint.

Shalini wrote the following on a piece of paper:

Blue	Yellow
2	3
4	6

Shalini: Can we work anything else out?
Ali: Well we could add another two scoops of blue paint to make six blue, and another three scoops of yellow to make nine yellow.
Ian: Or we could just double the amount of blue paint to get eight and double the amount of yellow paint to get twelve.
Shalini was surprised but pleased that Ian had made this connection and reported the incident back to the teacher, who was able to use it as an illustration in the next mathematics lesson.

Reflection on the case study
Shalini used the opportunity to explore ratio with the pupils in a real-life context. She supported their learning through her questioning and the drawing of the chart. This enabled both Ian and Ali to make connections and use equivalent ratios to solve the problem. Shalini recognised it had been a good learning experience and so shared the event with the teacher, who was then able to use it in her own teaching with the rest of the class.

Summary

This chapter has considered some very important ideas within mathematics and possibly challenged your own understanding. The themes of making connections and equivalence are also relevant to other areas of mathematics and are important to success in the subject. Other things to remember are:

- The need to assure pupils that struggling with mathematical ideas is part of the learning process, and they should not consider themselves failures if they do not instantly understand. Some of the greatest mathematicians spent years playing with ideas before they fully understood a concept!
- The importance of practical activities, resources and contexts to support and develop pupils' understanding.
- When working with pupils, remind them of other connected areas of learning that they have been involved in. This will support their learning by helping them to make links and build on previous knowledge.

Answers to the task

Fifths and their equivalent decimals and percentages

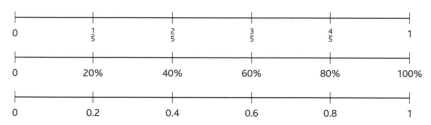

Thirds and their equivalent decimals and percentages

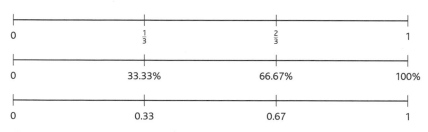

Note: because 100 does not divide equally by 3, the numbers have been rounded

References

Haylock, D. (2005) *Mathematics Explained for Primary Teachers*, third edition. London: Paul Chapman Publishing

Hopkins, C., Pope, S. and Pepperell, S. (2004) *Understanding Primary Mathematics*. London: David Fulton Publishers

8. Shape, space and measures

Introduction

With the introduction of the National Numeracy Strategy and its emphasis on number, it is easy for space, shape and measures to become neglected areas. These are, however, important and exciting areas of mathematics where there may be opportunities for some children who are weaker in number to succeed. It is important that your own subject knowledge is secure in this area so that you may more effectively support the pupils with whom you work.

HLTA STANDARDS

2.1 They have sufficient understanding of their specialist area to support pupils' learning, and are able to acquire further knowledge to contribute effectively and with confidence to the classes in which they are involved.

2.2 They are familiar with the school curriculum, the age-related expectations of pupils, the main teaching methods and the testing/examination frameworks in the subjects and age ranges in which they are involved.

2.3 They understand the aims, content, teaching strategies and intended outcomes for the lessons in which they are involved, and understand the place of these in the related teaching programme.

3.3.1 Using clearly structured teaching and learning activities, they interest and motivate pupils and advance their learning.

CHAPTER OBJECTIVES

By the end of this chapter you should:

● understand the main aims of the curriculum for shape, space and measures and the age-related expectations

● know the properties of common 2D and 3D shapes

● appreciate the importance of visualisation in relation to shape and space

● recognise the connections between number and measures.

Two-dimensional and three-dimensional shape in the curriculum

Shape is a natural part of the world around us; however, children do not necessarily relate shape within the natural environment to shape within the curriculum. When working with pupils you can support them in making the necessary connections.

2D shape is generally introduced first within the curriculum. There is an argument for introducing 3D first as it provides a more concrete experience for young children. 2D shape is in fact an abstract concept. Those plastic or wooden 2D shapes found in most classrooms represent 2D shapes but are not actually two-dimensional since they do have an element of thickness to them. 3D shapes can be handled, explored and used to build 3D models. While engaged in exploration, pupils can also experience 2D shape in terms of the flat faces of 3D shapes. For example, a cube has six square faces.

The emphasis within the shape curriculum should be directed at the properties of shape. An emphasis on properties provides pupils with opportunities to make connections between different shapes and classify them. It also enables them to analyse any shape, including irregular shapes. It is important that pupils are exposed to irregular shapes in order to expand their understanding. Often children will only relate shape to the models used to demonstrate within the school environment. If they are only exposed to regular shapes, such as a hexagon with six equal sides, then they will only recognise a hexagon by this predefined image. Irregular shapes challenge thinking and put the emphasis on identifying properties. Include irregular shapes in your work with pupils and draw attention to shapes within the real world.

Age-related expectations for shape and space are outlined in the NNS Framework, a summary of which is given below. Please note the list does not necessarily include every aspect of the shape and space curriculum but key aspects are outlined to demonstrate progression. The objectives have been divided into three separate strands. These exemplify progression in different areas of the shape and space curriculum. However, it is important to note that there is considerable overlap between these areas. These should give you an overview and support you in monitoring progress and providing feedback to the teacher.

Year			
R	Begin to name solids such as cube, cone, sphere and flat shapes such as square, triangle, and circle.	Recognise, talk about and recreate patterns.	Use everyday words to describe position.

1	Use everyday language to describe features, such as sides, faces, corners or edges of familiar 3D and 2D shapes.	Make and describe models, patterns and pictures.	Use everyday language to describe position, direction and movement. Make whole and half turns.
2	Use mathematical names for common 3D and 2D shapes such as pyramid, cylinder, pentagon and hexagon. Sort shapes and describe features such as sides, corners, faces and edges.	Make and describe shapes, pictures and pattern. Recognise line symmetry.	Use mathematical vocabulary to describe position, direction and movement. Recognise whole, half and quarter turns.
3	Classify and describe 3D and 2D shapes such as hemisphere, prism, semicircle and quadrilateral, including the identification of right angles.	Identify and sketch line symmetry in simple shapes.	Read and begin to write the vocabulary related to position, direction and movement. Make and describe right-angle turns.
4	Describe and visualise 2D and 3D shapes including tetrahedron and heptagon. Classify polygons according to their properties. Identify nets of simple solid shapes.	Sketch the reflection of a solid shape in a mirror line. Recognise position and direction on a numbered grid.	Make and measure clockwise and anti-clockwise turns.
5	Recognise properties of rectangles. Classify triangles. Identify different nets for an open cube (5 faces). Recognise perpendicular and parallel lines.	Make shapes with increasing accuracy. Recognise reflective symmetry in regular polygons. Recognise where a shape will be after translation.	Understand and use a protractor in degrees.
6	Describe and visualise properties of solid shapes such as parallel or perpendicular faces or edges. Classify quadrilaterals. Identify different nets for a closed cube (6 faces).	Recognise where a shape will be after reflection in two mirror lines. Recognise where a shape will be after rotation through 90° about one of its vertices.	Recognise and estimate angles. Use a protractor to measure and draw acute and obtuse angles to the nearest degree. Calculate angles in a triangle or around a point.

The language of shape and space

It is important that as a TA you are familiar with the language of shape and space so that you can model its use when working with pupils. A list of vocabulary for each year is provided in the *Mathematical Vocabulary* (DFEE 2000) booklet.

Language relating to shape may be considered complex as it is littered with Greek words, such as dodecahedron (a solid shape with 12 faces). However, children often love these technical words and they should not be avoided, even when working with lower-attaining pupils or pupils with special educational needs. Limiting vocabulary can often result in limiting understanding. It is therefore important that when working with pupils you not only encourage the use of technical language, but also through discussion ensure they are secure in its meaning. You will notice from the table above that everyday language is used first and then the mathematical language introduced to support progression in understanding.

Case study

Sue, a TA was working with a group of Year 3 pupils in the daily mathematics lesson. The topic was 3D shape.
Sue: Let's look at this shape (*holding up a cube*). Can any one tell me anything about it? What properties does it have?
Millie: It's red
Sue: Yes it is red; can anyone tell me anything else?
Ziggy: It has six sides.
Sue: What do you mean by six sides?
Ziggy: Like a square has four sides, it has six sides.
Sue: Can you show me where they are? (*Ziggy pointed in turn to the six faces on the cube.*)
Sue realised that Ziggy had confused sides and faces and reported this to the teacher.

Reflection on the case study

This is a common error and illustrates the need for precision in the use of mathematical language, as discussed in Chapter 4. The word 'side' in mathematics refers to an edge, whereas in everyday language the word 'side' can be used to refer to a surface, such as the side of a coin. This was the sense in which Ziggy was using it. The word 'edge' should be used when making reference to 3D shape and the word 'side' reserved for 2D shape only.

Properties of 2D shapes

A polygon is any 2D shape, completely enclosed by three or more straight sides. Therefore a triangle, square, rectangle, hexagon, etc., are all polygons.

Pupils are required to demonstrate understanding of the properties of these shapes in their ability to identify, sort and classify them. You should encourage pupils to reason and talk about the properties of shape in order to support learning.

Below is a list of polygons and their properties for your reference.

Polygon	A flat shape enclosed by 3 or more straight sides
Triangles	A polygon which has 3 sides. The sum of its interior angles is 180°
Equilateral	3 equal sides; 3 equal angles
Isosceles	2 equal sides; 2 equal angles
Scalene	0 equal sides; 0 equal angles
Quadrilaterals	A polygon which has 4 sides. The sum of its interior angles is 360°
Square	4 equal sides; 4 right angles; opposite sides equal and parallel; 4 lines of symmetry
Rectangle	4 right angles; opposite sides equal and parallel; 2 lines of symmetry
Oblong	4 right angles; length and breadth unequal, 2 lines of symmetry
Rhombus	4 equal sides; opposite sides equal and parallel; opposite angles equal, 2 lines of symmetry, the diagonals bisect at right angles
Parallelogram	2 pairs of opposite parallel sides, opposite sides equal, opposite angles equal
Kite	2 pairs of adjacent sides equal, 1 pair opposite angles equal, 1 line of symmetry
Trapezium	1 pair parallel sides
Other polygons	
Pentagon	5 sides, regular pentagons have equal sides and angles
Hexagon	6 sides, regular hexagons have equal sides and angles
Heptagon	7 sides, regular heptagons have equal sides and angles
Octagon	8 sides, regular octagons have equal sides and angles

PRACTICAL TASK

The aim of this task is to give you the opportunity to reason and explore shape using your knowledge of properties. Reflection on the strategies you use should give you an insight into how pupils learn.

Use the information above and your own reasoning, to answer the following questions:

1. Is it possible to draw a triangle with two right angles?

2. Is it possible to draw a right-angled isosceles triangle?

3. Is a square a rectangle?

4. Is a square a rhombus?

5. Is a rhombus a parallelogram?

6. Is it true that a trapezium has one line of symmetry?

Answers

1. It is not possible to draw a triangle with two right angles. Two right angles would total 180° and the lines would not join together to form a shape with three sides.

2. It is possible to draw a right-angled isosceles triangle, the other two angles would share the remaining 90° and thus be 45° each.

3. A square is a rectangle since it has all its properties, having four right angles with opposite sides equal and parallel. It is a special type of rectangle with the additional property of equal sides and therefore has its own name.

4. A square is a rhombus since it has all the properties of a rhombus. It is a special type of rhombus with the additional property of all the angles being 90°.

5. A rhombus is a parallelogram; it is a special type of parallelogram with equal sides.

6. A trapezium may have one line of symmetry. Where one pair of sides is parallel and the other pair of sides is equal, it forms an isosceles trapezium and has two pairs of equal angles and one line of symmetry. Other trapezia will have no lines of symmetry.

Reflection on the task

As you have seen, different shapes may share common properties. You were required to make links and connections between shapes, using your reasoning skills. When working with pupils you need to support them in doing the same by encouraging them to recognise and talk about the properties of shape. As part of your HLTA assessment you will need to demonstrate that you are able to use learning activities to advance learning. Including the element of reasoning within an activity will challenge pupils' thinking and provide rich opportunities for learning.

Properties of 3D shape

Shape	Properties
Polyhedron	A minimum of 4 faces, all faces are polygons, a regular polyhedron has identical faces and vertices: Cube — 6 squares Tetrahedron — 4 equilateral triangles Octahedron — 8 equilateral triangles Dodecahedron — 12 regular pentagons Icosahedron — 20 equilateral triangles
Cuboid	An irregular polyhedron; 6 faces that are all rectangles; 12 edges; 8 vertices
Pyramid	1 polygon base, all the other faces are triangular and taper to a point, called the apex
Prism	2 polygon ends the same shape and size, the other faces are all rectangular
Cylinder	2 equal circular faces at opposite ends; 1 curved surface
Sphere	1 curved surface, every point on its surface is the same distance from its centre. It forms a perfect ball
Cone	1 circular base and a curved surface that tapers to a point, called the apex

PRACTICAL TASK

The aim of this task is to enable you to explore 3D shape and secure your own subject knowledge.

Identify the shape:

1. It has four faces, all of which are the same?

2. It has two triangular faces and three rectangular faces?

3. It is a special type of prism with identical faces?

4. It has seven faces; two of which are opposite identical polygons and 15 edges.

5. It has six faces, five of the faces are identical and its net looks like a star?

Answers and reflection

1. A tetrahedron is also a pyramid as it meets the criteria of a polygon base and triangular faces tapering to a point. It is a special type of pyramid.

2. A triangular prism.

3. A cube is in fact a prism as it meets all the criteria. It can be viewed as having two polygon ends, both of which are square. The other faces are rectangular, since a square is a special type of rectangle.

▶

4. A pentagonal prism.

5. A pentagonal pyramid.

   Visualising the transformation of a net into its 3D solid is an important skill and is discussed below.

As part of your HLTA assessment you will need to demonstrate that you have sufficient understanding of your specialist area to support pupils' learning. Many practitioners lack confidence in some areas of mathematics. The important thing is that you take the time and opportunities available to further develop your own subject knowledge.

Visualisation in shape

The ability to visualise a shape and manipulate it mentally is an important skill. Any opportunities you have to engage pupils in such activities will be valuable to their development. The skill does not come instantly but needs practice and is developed over time. Test out your own visualisation skills by engaging in the activity below:

Which of these nets can be folded to construct a cube?

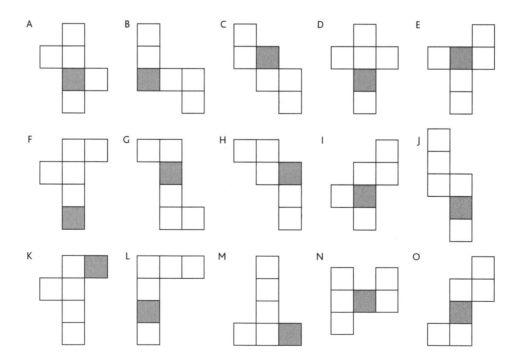

Ansell, B. (2005) *Numeracy Resources* CD

Answers

B, H, L, N are *not* nets of cubes. The other 11 are nets of cubes. There are in fact only 11 possible nets for a cube.

You may have found the activity quite challenging. Some people have greater visualisation skills than others. However, with practice everyone can develop, no matter what their age!

Measures in the curriculum

The measures curriculum has very close links with the number curriculum. As a TA you can highlight and remind pupils of those links when working with them. The ability to make connections, as stated elsewhere in this book, is a key to success in mathematics. The table below provides an overview of key objectives in the measures curriculum with links to the number curriculum.

Year	Mathematical idea in measures	Connections to number
R	Use language such as more or less, greater or smaller, heavier or lighter, to compare two numbers or quantities.	Comparative language is also used in number; for example, the use of more or less.
1	Suggest suitable standard or uniform non-standard units and measuring equipment to estimate, and then measure a length, mass or capacity.	Estimation is a key skill in number and engages pupils in thinking about and developing an appreciation of size or quantity.
2	Read a simple scale to the nearest labelled division including using a ruler to draw and measure lines to the nearest cm.	All scales are in fact number lines whether they are horizontal, vertical, curved or circular. The same skills are used in all of them; using what you know (the labelled divisions on a scale) to work out what you don't know (the unlabelled divisions).
3	Use units of time and know the relationship between them (second, minute, hour, day, week, month, year).	Although time is numerical, the relationship between units of time is different from and more complex than those encountered in other areas of mathematics. It operates in divisions of 60 (60 seconds in a minute, 60 minutes in an hour), then in divisions of 24 (24 hours in a day) and then in divisions of 7 (7 days in a week), etc. This complexity needs to be highlighted to pupils. Calculating time using a number line is often a successful strategy, using a bridging through 60 strategy (this is explored in the practical task).

3	Begin to use decimal notation for metres and centimetres.	As in number, an understanding of place value is essential.
4	Know and use the relationship between familiar units of length, mass and capacity.	The relationships involve multiples of 10, 100 or 1000.
5	Understand area measured in square centimetres (cm). Understand and use the formula length x breadth for the area of a rectangle.	The mathematics is the same as working with arrays for multiplication. A 3 × 4 array totals 12. The area of a rectangle which has a length of 4 cm and a breadth of 3 cm is 12 cm (3 cm x 4 cm = 3 rows of 4 cm = 12 cm).
6	Convert smaller to larger units (e.g. m to km, cm or mm to m, g to kg, ml to l) and vice versa.	Conversion within measures involves multiplying and dividing by 10, 100 and 1000. This can be done using a place value grid and moving the digits back and forth, e.g. 56 cm can be converted to metres by dividing by 100 and moving two places to the right to give 0.56 m.

PRACTICAL TASK

The aim of this task is to provide you with an opportunity to explore some areas of the measures curriculum.

1. Calculate the area and perimeter of the following shape

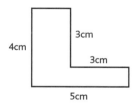

2. Fill in the table by converting each of the measurements into the specified units.
   Note: 10 millimetres = 1 centimetre; 100 centimetres = 1 metre;
   1000 metres = 1 kilometre

	mm	cm	m	km
10 cm				
1 km				
1 m				
1.2 m				
800 mm				

3. The record for the women's London Marathon is 2 hours 17 min. Runner 212 leaves the starting line at 10:37 and arrives at the finishing line at 13:04. Has she beaten the record?
    What is the difference between her time and the record time?
    Show your working on a number line.

4. Runner 213 starts at 10:52 and takes 3 hrs and 29 min. How long did he take to complete the race?
    Show your working on a number line.

Answers and reflection

1. Area = 11cm^2

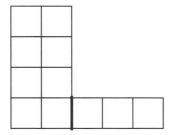

The shape needs to be divided into rectangles and each rectangle calculated in turn to find the area.

The first rectangle can be seen as a 4 by 2 array of square centimetres which total 8 square centimetres. This is where the formula length x breadth is derived from. 4 cm x 2 cm = 8 cm^2.
The second rectangle is 1 row of 3 square centimetres, 3 cm x 1 cm = 3 cm^2.
The final stage is to add the area of both rectangles together.
8 cm^2 + 3 cm^2 = 11 cm^2

A common misconception by pupils is to multiply 4 cm by 5 cm to equal 20 cm^2, using the formula length x breadth. This formula, of course, only works for rectangles, hence the need to first split the shape into rectangles. You may have split the shape in a different way creating a 3 x 2 array and a 1 x 5 array. Either way is acceptable.

To calculate the perimeter, first the missing dimensions need to be calculated using reasoning and the information known. The top of the L shape has a length of 2 cm and the missing side 1 cm.
Perimeter = 4 cm + 5 cm + 1 cm + 3 cm + 3 cm + 2 cm = 18 cm

Pupils often confuse area and perimeter. When working with them you may have the opportunity to talk and identify where the confusion is. This information gained is useful to feedback to the teacher who may then be able to plan suitable activities to develop understanding.

2.

	mm	cm	m	km
10 cm	100	10	0.1	0.0001
1 km	1 000 000	100 000	1000	1
1 m	1000	100	1	0.001
1.2 m	1200	120	1.2	0.0012
800 mm	800	80	0.8	0.0008

A place value grid where the digits are moved for multiplication by 10 and multiples of 10 is useful. This is discussed in greater detail in Chapter 7. There are 10 mm in 1 cm. Changing mm to cm requires a division of 10. Some pupils mistakenly think that multiplication is required since centimetres are bigger than millimetres. An easy way to think of it is to recognise that centimetres are bigger and so there will be fewer of them; therefore division is required.

3. Calculated using a number line:

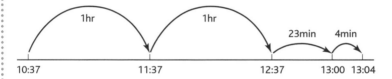

The time taken is 2 hours and 27 minutes, so runner 212 did not break the record, she missed it by 10mins.

4. Calculated using a number line:

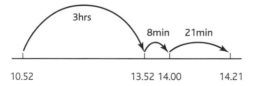

Runner 213 arrived at 14:21.

3 hrs is taken in one jump to reach a time of 13:52. The 29 mins is then partitioned into 8 and 21 to bridge through the next hr of 14:00. The remaining 21 mins is then easy to add on.

Time on a number line

Using a number line to solve problems involving time can be a very effective strategy.
Questions 3 and 4 represent the two types of time problem.
Question 3 asks for a time interval and the answer is 2 hrs and 27 min.

Question 4 asks for an actual time. In this case 14:21.

Note that the number lines have not been drawn to scale. The line is to support thinking and keep track of the calculations involved. You need to reassure pupils that their lines do not need to be drawn to scale.

Summary

- You should now have an overview and an understanding with regard to age-related expectations of the shape, space and measures curriculum.
- You should have developed your own subject knowledge of shape, space and measures and have an understanding of potential strategies used by pupils.
- It is important that you are aware of the links between the measures and number curriculum in order that you can support pupils in making these connections. This will make learning more effective.
- You should recognise the importance of visualisation of shape and the need to take opportunities for its development when working with pupils.

References and resources

DfEE (1999) *The National Numeracy Strategy, Framework for Teaching Mathematics from Reception to Year 6*

DfEE (2000) *Mathematical Vocabulary*. DfEE 0313-2000

Tapson F(1999) *Oxford Mathematics Study Dictionary*, Oxford University Press. This is a useful dictionary for your own reference.

www.atm.org.uk/resources/convexpolyhedra.html This site contains some useful 3D shape resources to develop your own subject knowledge and support your work with pupils.

Ansell, R. (2005) *Numeracy Resources CD* This resource can be purchased from the following website: www.numeracycd.com. It contains a large number of printable resources for Key Stages 1 and 2.

9. The use of ICT

Introduction

There has been a significant growth in the availability and use of ICT in primary classrooms in recent years. Such has been the investment that as a tool it cannot be ignored. It is important that all practitioners working within the classroom environment are confident and competent in its use. As a TA it is likely that you will at some point make use of ICT to support learning in mathematics. This may be in the form of a computer, a calculator, a programmable robot or data-logging equipment. You will also be involved in producing materials using ICT to support learning and the needs of individual pupils.

It is recognised that ICT does have significant potential in enhancing the learning of mathematics; however, this potential is not always realised. It takes considerable skill to know when and how to use it and to select appropriate software to support learning objectives. Many of these decisions will be made by the teacher, but often in conjunction with you as a TA. There will also be times when the teacher will delegate responsibility to you for selecting materials and resources, including ICT to support learning of an individual or group of pupils. You should develop a level of expertise in your knowledge of an increasing range of ICT programs and equipment and their potential to support learning.

HLTA STANDARDS

2.4   They know how to use ICT to advance pupils' learning, and can use common ICT tools for their own and pupils' benefit.

3.1.1 They contribute effectively to the selection and preparation of teaching resources that meet the diversity of pupils' needs and interests.

CHAPTER OBJECTIVES

By the end of this chapter you should:

● be able to select and assess ICT equipment and software in terms of its potential to support individual learning objectives

● understand when and how pupils should use a calculator

● understand how to use ICT to support pupils' independence in learning

● recognise the potential of ICT to support the teaching and learning of data handling.

Using a computer and selecting software

Computers can provide motivation, differentiation and access to the curriculum for pupils. There is a vast range of software now available, some of which is free to download from the internet. As a TA you may be involved in the selection of material to meet the needs of an individual or group of pupils. The following points need to be taken into consideration:

- Will it address the learning objectives?
- Is it sufficiently challenging to engage pupils in thinking and enable them to make progress?
- Will it motivate pupils? A program does not necessarily have to be sophisticated to engage interest. In fact programs which are too complex may not adequately focus on the learning intentions.
- Is it age appropriate? This may be particularly applicable for children with learning difficulties. The mathematics may be at a lower level, but this does not mean that the graphics should be patronising.

When pupils are engaged in using software you need to consider, whether they are actually learning or just having fun. Some programs may actually discourage pupils from thinking; for example, where a short time limit has been set to enter an answer. Pupils may guess at an answer, rather than using strategies and taking time to work it out.

Engaging pupils in discussion on what they are doing will gain you access to their thinking and the opportunity to assess learning. This information can then be used to inform your next step in providing support and also feedback to the teacher to inform their planning.

It is possible to produce your own material for use on the computer. Graphics can be cut and pasted into a PowerPoint file for counting, number recognition and to stimulate problem-solving activities. If you are familiar with Microsoft Excel you may wish to experiment with writing a simple program. There are some examples of programs on the National Interactive Whiteboard website.

Interactive teaching programmes and other DfES material

Alongside the government's commitment to the use of ICT is a bank of software, freely available to download from the Primary Strategy and the National Whiteboard Network websites. The *Interactive Teaching Programs* (ITPs) are simple programmes covering a wide range of mathematical topics. There are programmes suitable for all age ranges, including Foundation Stage through to Year 6. They are not designed for pupils to use alone, but with a teacher or TA who can then guide and direct the learning and create the necessary discussion and interaction. It may be that you use a program with a small group of pupils after demonstration by the teacher to the whole class, to provide reinforcement and consolidation; or that you select a program to meet the needs of an individual or group of pupils with whom you work. The opportunity for talk and discussion that can arise from these programs is especially valuable.

A package of software which was originally part of a training pack 'Using ICT to support mathematics in primary schools' is also available on the Primary Strategy website. *Counter* is a versatile program that can be used with all age ranges within the primary-school. It can be used for number recognition, multiples, exploring the number system and problem-solving. Suggestions for activities are available on Mathsweb, the Leicestershire website, referenced at the end of this chapter. The *function machine* can also be used at a variety of levels and provides opportunities for pupils to use reasoning to solve problems.

For exploring angles, 'What's my angle' demonstrates how to use a protractor for measuring and provides experience in estimating angles. 'Monty' is a fun program for exploring a 100 square and reasoning about number. Both these and the ITPs mentioned above will require familiarity before you use them with pupils. If they are not available in your school, ask for permission to download them to a computer so that you may explore them before use.

Interactive whiteboards

Interactive whiteboards are becoming standard equipment in the primary classroom. They may be used by the teacher on a regular basis as part of whole-class teaching but can also be used by small groups of pupils independently or with a TA. Research suggests that the physical interaction whereby pupils can touch the screen and move objects around is an important element in supporting learning. The opportunities, they provide for discussion and decision-making are also valuable. The National Whiteboard Network provides a website offering materials and advice to support their use, including health and safety guidance. As a TA you need to be aware of health and safety, such as where to position the projector when the whiteboard is in use.

Programmable floor robots

These are small robots that can be programmed to move in different directions. Some also make simple noises. They come in a variety of forms and some have the facility of inserting a pen so that the path of the robot can be traced. Suitable activities include programming the robot to follow a path or maze; or drawing shapes, starting with a square and progressing to more complex shapes, such as a five-pointed star. These activities give pupils opportunities to reason, problem solve, think logically, estimate and experience distance and angle. When working with pupils, allow them to experiment and make mistakes. Encourage them to learn from their mistakes in order to improve their programming skills and their knowledge of distance and angles.

Case study

Sarah is a TA who was working with two pupils in Year 2 working at level 2. The objectives for the session were to recognise right angles and estimate length. The task was to program the floor robot to visit four houses, each situated on the four corners of a rectangle.

Sarah: Where are you going to start?
Ali: Send him to the red house first, because he's facing that way.
Sarah: OK, what do you need to do first?
Ben: Well its forward, but I don't know how far.
Ali: I think it's about 10.
Sarah: 10 what?
Ali: 10 centimetres.
Sarah: OK then try it.
Sarah knew it was much further than 10 cm but she let Ali try out his idea.
Tom: Look, it's only gone a little way, so it's more than 10 cm.
Ali: OK let's try 20.
Tom: No, it's more than 20 because look it's more than two lots of 10 (*demonstrates with his hands*).
The two boys carry on their estimating until they get it right and reach the red house.
Ali: We need to turn the corner now.
Sarah: Tom can you tell us how to do that?
Tom: Well I guess it's that button (*pointing to the arrow with a right-hand turn*).
Tom pressed it and nothing happened.
Sarah: You have to tell it the size of the turn
Tom: I don't know.
Sarah: Well try something.
Tom tried 10 and then 50, before Ali spotted a poster on the wall.
Tom: It's a right angle so it must be 90.
Sarah: That's right, it's 90 degrees.

The activity continued with the boys eventually recording their program and executing it in one go.

Reflection on the case study
Sarah allowed the pupils to investigate their ideas, even though she knew that sometimes these were wrong. This enriched the learning and met the learning objectives in developing estimating skills both for length and angle.

Data-logging equipment

This is equipment that records changes in variables over time. Data logging is used in the real world, for example in recording cars entering and leaving a car park. This information is useful as it can calculate the number of spaces available at any given moment in time. In the primary classroom it can be used to detect sound or pulse rate, changes in temperature, mass and light.

Often these are difficult for primary age pupils to record with accuracy. The data-logging equipment can enable the data to be analysed and allow pupils to reason and draw conclusion. Obviously there are strong links here with the science curriculum. If the equipment is available in your school you need to become familiar with how it operates.

Calculators

The use of a calculator for calculation is not recommended in the NNS Framework until towards the end of Key Stage 2, since the emphasis is on developing mental calculation skills. However, it is a valuable tool to explore and develop understanding of number. Used in this way it can be explored as early as the Foundation Stage. A calculator with a large key pad and display is a valuable resource in a Reception classroom. It can be used in a role-play area where the tapping in of numbers can support number recognition and counting.

PRACTICAL TASK

The aim of this task is to enable you to consider the strategies pupils might use and the role of the calculator to solve the problem.

Using the digits 1 to 5 only, investigate the maximum product that can be formed. You must use all the digits each time.

$$\boxed{}\ \boxed{}\ \boxed{}\ \times\ \boxed{}\ \boxed{}\ =\ ?$$

Reflection on the activity

It is likely that you used your knowledge of place value and placed the 5, the highest digit, in the first position of one of the numbers and used similar reasoning for the other digits. Recording of your work and discounting arrangements of digits as larger products were found, would also have helped.

This type of activity allows pupils to work with larger numbers and enables them to try things out with ease, while gaining an insight into the mathematics involved. In this example it gave the opportunity for place value and multiplication to be explored. The calculator can enable pupils to focus on problem-solving without the calculation getting in the way.

The development of calculator skills is not mentioned in the NNS Framework until Year 5. However, if you are working with pupils who are using calculators, for example in the type of activity described above, then you need to ensure that they are confident in their use. Ensure that they are hitting the keys with enough pressure to ensure entry. Some pupils with special educational needs may require a calculator with larger keys, or one which does not require as much pressure. You can observe how a pupil is coping and provide feedback to the teacher. Ensure also that they are able to operate the basic functions of the calculator, such as the operation keys and clear entry and clear all. They may also be required to use the constant function in some classroom activities. This allows the calculator to produce a string of numbers using a constant operation, such as add 2 where the numbers 2, 4, 6, 8, 10... are produced by repeated hitting the Entry or Equals key. This provides the opportunity for the exploration of number patterns and sequences.

Try this out on your calculator:

This should produce 3, 6, 9 and will continue to produce multiples of three with the repeated striking of the Equals key. However, calculators vary and it may be that you only needed to press the addition key once. If this doesn't work then refer to the instruction manual for your particular calculator.

Where pupils have access to calculators for calculation, you need to support them in making decisions as to when its use is appropriate. You should encourage them to consider first whether they can complete the calculation mentally, and if not whether a formal written method or a calculator is required. Eventually these should be decisions which pupils make for themselves. Your support should be directed at developing pupils' independence in making the right decision. Talk to them about the numbers involved and the possible strategies they could use.

Using ICT to support data handling

The focus of data handling in the primary curriculum is to 'solve a problem by collecting, organising, representing, extracting and interpreting data in tables, graphs and charts' (NNS Framework Section 6, page 114). The NNS Framework outlines a clear progression from Reception through to Year 6. In Reception pupils may sort and count themselves, responding to a criterion, such as all those who have brown eyes, are wearing black shoes, are five years old etc. In Year 6 the expectations are that pupils will be able to find the mode and range of a simple set of data and draw and interpret line graphs.

The cycle of data handling to solve a problem has five stages:

1. Identify the problem.
2. Plan what data is needed and how it will to be collected.
3. Collect the data.
4. Process and represent the data.
5. Interpret the data.

Pupils will not go through this whole process every time data handling is addressed in the curriculum, but the focus will be on different elements at different times. The use of ICT can be particularly valuable in the final three elements.

Although it is useful for pupils to collect their own data, this can be time consuming and does not have to happen every time data is collected. Secondary data can be collected using the internet and the school census website is useful for this purpose. This site has information collected from school children across the world and includes details such as their height, their pets and how they travel to school. The website also includes activities and data can be tailored to suit the needs and age ranges of pupils.

Drawing graphs can also take time and it needs to be considered whether colouring in a bar chart is a useful mathematical activity in terms of learning. Some pupils may also struggle with the accuracy required in drawing their own graphs. Software which produces instant graphs from data is a valuable tool. Attention can then be given to discussion and interpretation of the information the graph provides. Interpretation of graphs is an important skill and should be a key focus within the curriculum for data handling.

An additional ICT tool that can be used to collect data is a voting device. This is used in conjunction with the interactive whiteboard and can in seconds collect data from the class and produce a graph. Each pupil has a voting device and a question is displayed on the interactive whiteboard. For example, 'How do you travel to school: a. walk, b. ride a bike, c. travel by car, d. travel by bus?' Pupils enter the letter of the appropriate answer on the keypad of their voting device. This data is recorded by the computer and a graph can be displayed on the screen, ready for analysis and interpretation.

Summary

- At whatever stage you are in your ICT competence, you should seek to continue to develop and keep up to date in your skills.
- ICT has significant potential to enhance learning; however, careful selection and application is required. When working with pupils using ICT, you should ask yourself: are pupils actually learning or could the ICT be getting in the way? If it is the latter then this needs to be discussed with the teacher.
- ICT can promote discussion. Take advantage of this when working with pupils.

References and resources

Census at school: **www.censusatschool.ntu.ac.uk**
This is an international school census website; any school is welcome to take part. Even if your school is not a member you still have access to data and activities. It is aimed primarily at Key Stages 2 and 3.

Interactive Teaching Programs (ITPs) and other software
www.standards.dfes.gov.uk/primary/publications/mathematics/itps
The ITPs address a wide range of mathematical topics. Also available is the
software from the 'Using ICT to support mathematics in primary schools' pack.

National Whiteboard Network **www.nwnet.org.uk**
Advice and resources for Interactive Whiteboards

ICT advice site **www.ictadvice.org.uk**
Information on the selection and use of ICT across all curriculum subjects.

Becta **www.becta.org.uk** is the government's key partner in the development of
ICT within education. The site contains advice and the latest research on the use
of ICT in schools.

Mathsweb is the Leicestershire Numeracy website. It is easier to locate by typing
Mathsweb into a reliable search engine. Within the primary teachers section are
ideas for activities using the program counter.

National Curriculum in Action www.ncaction.org.uk/index.htm
This site has examples of pupils' work where ICT is used to support mathematics,
including examples of data logging.

Ref: NNS930 DfES, *(2001) Calculator Activities*
www.standards.dfes.gov.uk/primary/publications
This document provides a number of calculator activities, most of which are of a
problem-solving nature.

10. Mathematics across the curriculum and within the environment

Introduction

Mathematics is an important life skill and learning should not be confined to the structured mathematics lesson. There are valuable opportunities to apply and see mathematics in real-life contexts both outside of the classroom and within other curriculum subjects. It is important that you are aware of mathematics and its skills in other subjects. This will support you in maximising learning opportunities for the pupils with whom you work. Pupils do not readily transfer their skills across other subjects and often need prompting to make connections. All schools support out-of-schools visits and see these as valuable both academically and socially. As a TA you can support the teacher in researching and planning opportunities for learning within mathematics and other subjects.

HLTA STANDARDS

2.2   They are familiar with the school curriculum, the age-related expectations of pupils, the main teaching methods and the testing/examination frameworks in the subjects and age ranges in which they are involved.

2.5   They know the key factors that can affect the way pupils learn.

3.1.4   They are able to contribute to the planning of opportunities for pupils to learn in out-of-school contexts in accordance with school policies and procedures.

CHAPTER OBJECTIVES

By the end of this chapter you should:

- recognise opportunities outside of the classroom to support learning within mathematics
- recognise mathematics as a cross-curricular skill
- recognise opportunities for developing learning of mathematics, across the curriculum.

Mathematics in other subjects

The National Curriculum recognises the application of number as a cross-curricular skill. Indeed there are aspects of some subjects which cannot function without the application of mathematics. Consider the nature of science: the links with mathematics are numerous. It requires the skill of measuring, counting, calculating, recognising pattern, working with variables and formulae, sorting and classifying. Even a subject such as history has some mathematics within it, in the form of time lines and sequencing. Pointing out to pupils that a time line is another form of a number line gives them an insight and develops understanding.

PRACTICAL TASK

The aim of this practical task is for you to explore opportunities for the application of mathematics in other subjects.

Select two curriculum areas and for each subject list the possible use of mathematics within these subjects.

Reflection on the task

Thinking about the presence of mathematics in other subjects may have surprised you. There are many opportunities you may not have thought about before. Many pupils do not automatically make these connections and may require prompting in order to appreciate the link. As a TA you can play a part in this and enhance their learning. Below are some suggestions of mathematics in other subjects; you may have thought of other ideas.

Geography involves measurements and distances using standard units of measurement. It also involves routes and pathways and exploring shape and space.

Art can involve ratio in the mixing of paint and exploring colour. Shape and space can also be explored as well as the use of lines, symmetry and pattern.

Design technology involves measurement and consideration of shape and space in the construction of models and other objects.

Physical education involves time and distances and can also involve symmetry and the exploration of shape and space, for example in dance. A good activity for young pupils is to explore a route around an obstacle course, using positional language. This gives meaning to the language as they climb over, under and through objects.

ICT is used as a mathematical tool, as discussed in Chapter 9. It also involves the mathematical skills of reasoning and logical thinking as in programming a programmable robot.

Music has strong links with mathematics and is constructed through counting, time and pattern.

Case study

Kryza is a Year 2 child who is conscientious and above average ability in literacy. She is able to read and write well with neatness and precision. The teacher has noticed, however, that her progress in mathematics is slow. The teacher asked Peter, the TA, to observe her in the daily mathematics lessons and carry out some informal assessments. Peter noticed that when the class were counting in tens in an oral and mental starter, Kryza was finding it difficult to join in; the same was true when counting in fives and twos. The same day he also noticed in the music lesson that Kryza was having difficulty in clapping rhythm patterns and keeping time. He later discussed this with the teacher. Together they realised that Kryza had difficulty in recognising pattern. The teacher allocated Peter to work with Kryza to give additional practice on developing her ability to recognise pattern both in mathematics and music.

Reflection on the case study

The recognition of pattern features strongly both in mathematics and music. Seeing pattern is an inbuilt natural human ability; however, in some people, such as Kryza, it may not be strong. Peter's observations across the curriculum enabled him to see that this skill was weak and was affecting both subjects. This was addressed through an IEP with additional practice given in this area to support development.

Mathematics trails

Mathematics trails take a particular route around a specified area, requiring problems to be solved along the way. They are intended to engage pupils in fun and motivating activities. They often require a significant amount of planning and creativity, but can then be repeated with different groups of pupils in subsequent years. As a TA you can be involved in supporting the teacher in planning such an activity. Your engagement in supporting pupils in completing the trail will also be valuable. Below are a few ideas to get you started, but the scope is vast and they can be tailored to fit into any mathematical or cross curricular topic.

A mathematical trail around the school

Start at the classroom door

> How tall is the door?
>
> If one child stood on another's shoulders, would they be able to walk through the door without bending down?

Walk down the corridor

> How many lights are in the corridor?
>
> If each light lasts 500 hours, how often will each light need replacing?

Go out into the playground

> What is the highest number on the number snake?
>
> What size of equal jumps could you make and still land on the last number?

Obviously the questions will be tailored to the age of the pupils involved. For younger pupils the trail can be presented in picture format with numbers of objects or shapes or patterns to be identified. Measurement can be included using non-standard measurement such as measuring the length of the school hall by the number of footsteps. Questions may also be differentiated with alternative questions given to groups of pupils. In the pairs of questions above, the first is easier than the second. It may therefore be possible for pupils to work in mixed ability groups. The questions are intended to create discussion and involve pupils in practical exploration. The last question above should involve children jumping along the numbers snake and exploring factors of the highest number on the snake. Key points from these discussions can be drawn together on return to the classroom. Maths trails can be carried out in any setting, using the environment as a stimulus for questions.

Take a walk

Any activity which involves a walk can be used to observe and promote mathematical thinking. Consider the richness of pattern in the environment. Look at the overlapping pattern of roof tiles; are they all the same, why do they overlap? Shape and pattern are all around us. The different shapes of windows and the symmetry created in their construction are areas for discussion. Number is also present, on houses, buses and car number plates. Drawing pupils' attention to these things and perhaps challenging them through a simple investigation, such as how many different numbers can you make from the three digits on a particular car number plate, can enrich and make learning fun. Photographs taken during the walk can be taken back and used in the classroom.

Mathematics from pictures

Other environments can be brought into the classroom through the use of pictures and photographs. A photograph of a sunset, for example, could stimulate discussion on time and an investigation into the time the sun sets on different days and at different times of the year. This information is readily available on the internet and is referenced at the end of the chapter. For younger pupils a picture of people standing at a bus stop can create an imaginary situation where pupils can role-play the characters getting on and off the bus. This can involve counting, addition and subtraction. Alternatively the local playground can be brought inside through a photograph and the shapes created by the climbing frame and other apparatus explored. Obviously this does not replace a visit to the playground, but this is not always possible. When working with individual pupils, pictures can be selected according to their particular interests to motivate and engage them in mathematics.

Case study

The pupils in a Reception class went on a trip to a farm as part of a topic on animals. They took digital cameras with them so that they could take photographs of the animals to record the event and stimulate discussion on return to the classroom. Raheela, a TA, walked her group around the farm, engaging the children in discussion about the animals and helping them to take photographs. While they were observing some baby chicks scratching around their enclosure, she noticed that Sam was not watching the chicks but was instead looking at the fencing surrounding the enclosure, putting his fingers through and tracing the shapes it made. Raheela suggested to Sam that he took a photograph of the fence. On returning to the classroom the photographs were printed using the computer. Raheela pointed out Sam's photograph of the fence to the teacher. The teacher asked Sam if he wanted to take a photograph of the fence surrounding the school. Raheela supported Sam in doing this. They also took photographs of two different school gates. This lead to the unlikely topic of fences, and other photographs were collected. They created much discussion on shape and pattern and provided the stimulus for some art work.

Reflection on the case study

Raheela gave Sam the opportunity to pursue something that interested him. This provided a valuable learning opportunity not just for Sam but for the rest of the class. Sometimes the most unlikely photograph can stimulate interest and be used to support learning in mathematics.

Summary

- As a TA you should be aware and sensitive to opportunities to promote pupils' skills not just within the mathematics curriculum but across and outside the formal curriculum.

- Cross-curricular work can enrich the curriculum. You can play a valuable role in researching and suggesting ideas for cross-curricular work.

- Making connections across the curriculum can enrich learning. Many pupils do not automatically see the links. You should look for possible connections so that you can prompt and support pupils in making these connections.

References and resources

Meaningful Maths Trails

www.nrich.maths.org Go to the search button and type in the above title. This will take you to an article which has ideas and suggestions for conducting your own maths trail and visiting historic sites and places of interest which have their own mathematics trails.

Excellence and Enjoyment: learning and teaching in the primary years. DfES Publications (2004) Ref: 0524-2004. This training pack contains booklets, videos and CD-ROMs. It addresses and promotes the development of skills across the curriculum.

www.**ncaction.org.uk** This website provides examples of pupils' work. Some cross-curricular links are included, such as the use of ICT in mathematics and creativity across the curriculum.

www.**sunrisesunset.com** This site gives the sunrise and sunset times for the current calendar month.

Index

Higher Level Teaching Assistants

These practical guides provide a helpful combination of theory and practice for all teaching assistants on training and assessment routes to Higher Level Teaching Assistant status. The books are cross-referenced to the HLTA standards throughout, and include case studies, practical tasks and references to key theory and research. They emphasise the increasingly professional approach of teaching assistants working in modern classrooms. You can find out more information on each of these titles by visiting our website: www.learningmatters.co.uk

Becoming a Primary Higher Level Teaching Assistant
Richard Rose
160pp ISBN 10: 1 84445 025 2 ISBN 13: 978 1 84445 025 1

Becoming a Higher Level Teaching Assistant: Primary English
Jean Edwards
128pp ISBN 10: 1 84445 046 5 ISBN 13: 978 1 84445 046 6

Becoming a Higher Level Teaching Assistant: Primary Mathematics
Debbie Morgan
112pp ISBN 10: 1 84445 043 0 ISBN 13: 978 1 84445 043 5

Becoming a Higher Level Teaching Assistant: Primary Special Educational Needs
Mary Doveston, Steve Cullingford-Agnew
128pp ISBN 10: 1 84445 052 X ISBN 13: 978 1 84445 052 7